THE ANCIENT PATH

THE ANCIENT PATH

Old Lessons from the Church Fathers for a New Life Today

JOHN MICHAEL TALBOT

with Mike Aquilina

IMAGE

New York

Published in the United States by Image, an imprint of the
Crown Publishing Group, a division of Random House LLC,
a Penguin Random House Company, New York.
www.crownpublishing.com

IMAGE is a registered trademark and the "I" colophon is a trademark of
Random House LLC.

Library of Congress Cataloging-in-Publication Data
is available upon request.

ISBN 978-0-8041-3995-3
eBook ISBN 978-0-8041-3996-0

Printed in the United States of America

Book design by Lauren Dong
Map by Christopher Bailey/Serif Press
Jacket design by Kristen Vasgaard
Jacket artwork: Bridgeman Art Library
Author photographs: (John Michael Talbot) Peggy Lodewyks;
(Mike Aquilina) Marie-Catherine Photography, Malibu, California

1 3 5 7 9 10 8 6 4 2

First Edition

Dedicated to the memory of Father Martin Wolter, OFM,
my spiritual father in the Church and in monastic life,
who pointed me to the early Church Fathers

CONTENTS

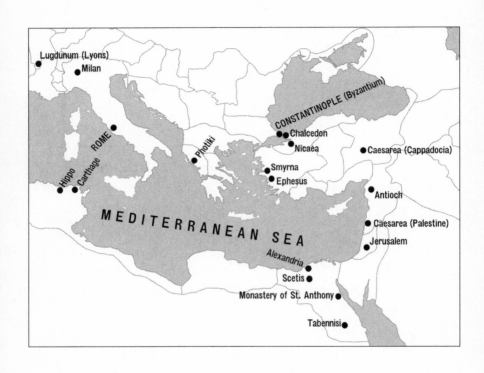

Lugdunum (Lyons)
Milan
CONSTANTINOPLE (Byzantium)
Chalcedon
ROME
Nicaea
Photiki
Caesarea (Cappadocia)
Hippo
Carthage
Smyrna
Ephesus
Antioch
MEDITERRANEAN SEA
Caesarea (Palestine)
Jerusalem
Alexandria
Scetis
Monastery of St. Anthony
Tabennisi

FOREWORD

JOHN MICHAEL TALBOT is best known as a musician and composer. But he is also a writer, builder, and founder of an integrated monastic community. As a Catholic layman, he is a devoted husband, father, and grandfather. He has exercised these roles in the latter part of the twentieth century and the early part of the twenty-first. Yet he has drawn inspiration for each of these diverse roles from authors who wrote many centuries ago. John's life and work have been shaped by the Fathers of the Church.

With all of the sociological studies, scientific writings, and theological reflections available today, what makes this book—which reaches back over centuries for its inspiration—such a valuable and engaging work?

There are ultimate and basic questions that each person at some point confronts, and these questions do not change over time. What is the meaning and purpose of life? How do I relate to God? How shall I live? These are always with us. As we look for wisdom to guide us, among the most enlightening and most convincing voices are those found in the writings of the Fathers of the Church. These are our ancestors in the faith, the remote founders of the Christian heritage that is ours today. We, a pilgrim people traveling through an often confusing secular society, are always in need of direction, encouragement, and good example.

The American philosopher George Santayana said: "Those who cannot remember the past are condemned to repeat it." If these words have any meaning—and I think we need to agree they do—then we must look to the past for much of our direction, encouragement, and good example. John Michael Talbot's book *The Ancient Path* does just that. It is directed primarily at adults today who would enjoy a popular narrative of the life and teaching of the early Fathers of the Church. Rather than a classroom or technical analysis, this easily readable book provides a profile of the Fathers and highlights why their wisdom should continue to be an inspiration for us today.

In reading *The Ancient Path*, I could not help but think of the great patristic scholar Father Johannes Quasten, whose multivolume *Patrology* is still a standard reference in the field. Father Quasten and I collaborated, together with other colleagues, on a catechism entitled *The Teaching of Christ*. He made sure that the Fathers were cited authoritatively and as often as possible. It was his emphasis on the Fathers that helped make that catechism such a beautiful reflection of the faith, well grounded in the Church's tradition. His focus was something I tried to carry with me after our work together was completed. Now comes John Michael Talbot's work on the Fathers, which, once again, opens up for us the depth of their understanding of the faith. Thus the richness of their spirituality continues to shed light on the path of Christians seeking to walk with the Lord.

Among the many outstanding features of this book—and

one for which it can be recommended to clergy as well as laity—is Talbot's ability to portray the humanity of the Church Fathers. The author's clear, engaging, yet concise style is at its best when he is describing the human qualities and characteristics of the early Church heroes as well as the people with whom they were associated.

The language of the Fathers sometimes seems archaic to us today, as do their cultural markers. Technology has changed so much in our day-to-day living. Yet human nature has not changed. Humanity still struggles against the same deadly sins, and we still strive to attain the same virtues. Jesus Christ remains the answer to the longings of the human heart, and the Fathers preached him most eloquently.

They evangelized a world and converted it in the course of just a few centuries. I daresay we have something to learn from them. The Acts of the Apostles tells us that before Jesus returned to his Father in glory, he charged his disciples, "You will be my witnesses" (Acts 1:8). That same mission echoes in our ears and hearts today. It was made clear at the Synod for the New Evangelization for the Transmission of the Christian Faith, which met in Rome in October 2012, that the continuation of the mission of Christ the Redeemer, which began with the great commissioning following his death and resurrection, is something that all of us are called to do today.

We are challenged not only to participate in the life of the Church, but actually to manifest the coming of God's kingdom in our world, and so to grow in spiritual stature. The call is to bring all things to Christ and make this temporal order a truly blessed expression of God's love, truth, and justice.

Throughout *The Ancient Path*, we find this same urgency and commitment. This short but powerful reflection on the wisdom of the Church Fathers invites us into the ongoing mission of spreading the Good News.

For two millennia, it has been the work of the whole Church, all the people of God, every member of the Body of Christ, to show forth to the world the presence of our Savior and Lord— who is one of us and is also the Son of God. We are called to be, in our lives, an epiphany of the Lord to those we encounter, a bright, shining light so that others might be led to him. We are called to be like the great star of Bethlehem that led the wise men to Jesus on that glorious Christmas day.

The kingdom of God that the Church Fathers sensed so poignantly offers humankind a different way of seeing life and the world around us. Christ points us to a fuller vision of life than that offered by the secular society that lives as if God did not exist. This was true in the very beginnings of the Church, often manifested in the days of the Fathers, and the task of pointing out the way has been a challenge of the Church for twenty centuries. In the Sermon on the Mount we hear of a new way of life—a way of beatitude—one that involves the merciful, those who hunger and thirst for righteousness, those who mourn, the peacemakers, the poor in spirit (Matthew 5:3-16). Reflecting upon this Good News gives us a whole new way of looking at life. John Michael Talbot sheds light on this path in his reflections on the lives of the Fathers. Our new way of seeing life through the lens of the Gospel, through the lens of the Fathers, offers us hope, stirring within us expectations of a fuller life and a better world.

The Fathers continue to speak to what is best in us. It is a joy to find them so easily accessible in these pages. John Michael Talbot has done us all a great favor by opening up the great gift of the Fathers. In his own unique style he has produced a splendid window looking out on the wisdom and the world of the Fathers. This work is a true blessing.

—His Eminence Cardinal Donald Wuerl,
Archbishop of Washington

Preface

P EOPLE OFTEN IMAGINE THE FATHERS OF THE Church looked like their icons and smelled like incense. They dream of heroic figures wrapped in fine liturgical vestments of silk and lace, engulfed in billows of smoke from their golden censers. But, truth be known, the men we meet in these writings often appear wearing the tattered cloak of Jesus or the dusty sweat-soaked habits of the Desert Fathers and Mothers. Theirs is an utterly incarnational spirituality. It is heaven-sent, but it moves forward with both feet on the ground of the earth.

They don't form a nice, neat package of Catholicism—though all the essential elements of the faith can be found in their writings. They write from the midst of challenge, conflict, and crisis. They were usually in a hurry, pressed for time, and they were writing for the moment more than for the ages.

From the hindsight of centuries, moderns might think the Fathers are "ultraconservative." They sure look old from here. But that's not true. They sought faithfully to conserve the deposit of truth passed on to them from Jesus through the apostles. But our categories of conservative and liberal are really alien to a correct understanding of the ancient past—and to the Catholic Church.

The Fathers, like all good Catholics, are neither ideologically conservative nor ideologically liberal. We are slaves to no Gospel but that of Jesus Christ. Rather, the Fathers were *radical*—from the Latin *radix*, for "root." They were rooted deeply in Jesus, the apostles, and the prophets. Both "conservatives" and "liberals" of late antiquity found ways to depart from the data of revelation. But the Fathers stood firm. They were not afraid to apply new language in new ways to describe ancient truths. Those who wanted to maintain ancient language alone always fell to the wrong side of history. Nor were the Fathers rigorists or spiritualists, though they often came from the disciplined environment of desert monasticism.

The First Epistle of Saint Peter tells us that we are a spiritual temple built of "living stones." The early Church Fathers represent the first rows built upon the foundation of the apostles. And that sacred building project continues throughout history to our time today. But it rests on the Fathers. It depends on them.

We'll see how that happens in the pages that follow.

———

This book grew out of conversations I had with my friend Mike Aquilina over the course of a week in November of 2012. It was my pleasure to give my guest the grand tour, hiking on long trails I helped to blaze in the dense forest hillsides around Little Portion Monastery in Arkansas.

Who knew that walks through the woods in Arkansas could make two very modern Americans (smartphones in pocket) experience such a profound communion with the ancient Fathers of the Church?

Who knew that the trails I blazed in the Ozarks could become for us an ancient path, simply through conversation?

We brought our conversation from the trails to the small living area of my hermitage, and Mike expanded on the topic in a series of conferences he gave for members of our monastic community and some local friends.

At some point during the week we just assumed that our conversations would become a book. I'm still not sure how that happened.

Mike has written many books on the Church Fathers. I asked him if he would help me to pull together *my* book on the Fathers—to tell the story of how the great teachers of the first millennium have shaped my life and work.

This book, then, is not a work of apologetics, much less systematic theology. It is not a comprehensive guide to the Fathers—or even a complete introduction. It is the story of one man's walk with Christ, accompanied by the Fathers, along the ancient path that all Christians are meant to travel.

I wanted to share, with as many readers as possible, the sense of discovery I got when I first cracked open a book of the Fathers. I wanted to communicate the excitement I feel when I go back to those books and read them for the second, third, or tenth time.

The Fathers were those who first issued the call we hear so often echoed by Pope Francis in our own day: "I invite all Christians, everywhere, at this very moment, to a renewed personal encounter with Jesus Christ."[1]

It has been a joy to walk along the Fathers' ancient path. It is a pleasure today to have you join me for the hike.

I gratefully acknowledge the good work of my friends at Image Books—in Colorado Springs and in New York City—who encouraged both Mike and me to keep the conversation going.

A NOTE ON SOURCES

Throughout this book I've drawn texts from several different editions of the Fathers. The translations I've used most often are in the nineteenth-century *Ante-Nicene Fathers* and *Nicene and Post-Nicene Fathers* series. I have almost always modernized the language.

Chapter 1

You Can Become All Fire

THE MONASTERY WHERE I LIVE, LITTLE PORTION Hermitage, nestles in a wooded valley off a rural route in the Ozark Mountains of northern Arkansas. Our community lives in solitude, far from the nearest streetlights or porch lights. At night the sky is filled with stars, and you can count them if you have the time. Our woods, though, are so dark that you can't see much beyond two feet in front of you.

In such a place, with such deep, dark nights, you come to appreciate the force of the Gospel's simple observation "It was night" (see John 13:30; also John 3:2). Night is the time when the wild beasts enjoy their brief advantage over human intelligence. They can see us; we can't see them. They can move easily through the terrain. Our every footfall is a guess—and a potential pratfall.

April 29, 2008, was just such a night. It was after eleven, and I was wrapping up my tasks for the day, a bit later than usual. My wife, Viola, was already asleep in bed. Our hermitage, like all the homes at the monastery, is a "green" building. Partially underground, it retains heat well in the winter and keeps pleasantly cool in the summer. Its great source of light by day is a skylight in the roof.

It was something about the skylight that startled me when I looked up from my desk. It should have been black with the night, but it was radiant—with a golden-orange glow.

Well, that's really strange, I thought.

My tired mind reached for implausible explanations as I headed for the door. *Maybe there's a problem with the well, and the utility crew is working late.*

Just three steps beyond my door I knew that the glow was nothing so benign. I felt intense heat. And I looked up to see the whole back end of the common building of our community— just a hundred yards from my hermitage—engulfed in flames.

The golden glow I had seen in the skylight? It was the immolation of our chapel, our library, our business offices, and the refectory where we share our simple meals.

—

My community is the Brothers and Sisters of Charity, and we have been living together since 1979, first on the grounds of Alverna Retreat Center in Indianapolis, and then, since 1982, on our grounds in Arkansas. We built the structures with our own hands from native stone and good wood. We built the *community* with similarly seasoned materials—the heritage of early Christianity, the traditions of Christian communal life. So we built our monastery as much with books as with blocks.

We weren't born in the valley where we now live. We converged there, came intentionally as disciples. The road we took was not just that rural route in the Ozarks, but a far more ancient path, the way of the Fathers.

We are a community that integrates families, singles who are free to marry, and traditional consecrated celibates. Our configuration is rare, if not unique, in modern times. But we fashioned it on models we found in the fourth century, when Christians in many lands undertook great experiments in living common life. Even as we built our buildings, we pored over the long-ago eyewitness accounts of the lives of Anthony of the Desert, Pachomius, John Cassian, Basil the Great, and the Fathers of the Egyptian desert. They and their companions fled the cities of the Greco-Roman world in order to make communities for intentional contemplative living. They succeeded so well—and built so sturdily—that many of their monasteries are still standing today, in spite of persecutions, and in spite of many centuries of natural disasters (what the insurance companies call "acts of God").

You can also see "monuments" of those ancient builders in the later experiments of Bernard of Clairvaux, Francis of Assisi, Dominic de Guzmán, and Ignatius of Loyola. The saints depend upon the saints; the Fathers took up what the apostles had handed on; the apostles learned the ways of common life from Jesus.

From the first generation it has been so. "And they devoted themselves to the apostles' teaching and fellowship, to the breaking of bread and the prayers. . . . And all who believed were together and had all things in common and they sold their possessions and goods and distributed them to all, as any had need" (Acts 2:42, 44-45).

If you spotted the ancient monasteries from a helicopter high above, you would be looking down on an ancient Christian commentary on the Scriptures. If you took a few turns and flew over Little Portion Hermitage, you could look down at our own particular reflection on the Gospel. We built the Gospel, as we saw it, into the layout of our roads and roofs.

Our monastery, as I said, consists of a large common building, surrounded by small habitations—hermitages—where individuals and families pass their days in quiet work and prayer and in solitude with God.

—

Maybe you can imagine, then, what passed through my mind in the instant when I recognized what was happening to our common building at the monastery. I stepped out of my hermitage to see the work of so many years, the work of our hearts and minds and hands, going up in flames.

At first I thought I would rush in and save what I could from the chapel. But I saw right away that the flames rose highest in the back end. The chapel—with its altar, tabernacle, and the choir stalls where we pray—was already gone. The vestments and vessels used in the sacred liturgy were gone. The icons were gone. So was my office, with all the community's records from thirty years of family life, and the awards and mementos of forty years of making music, and every photograph I had of my childhood, my late parents, my past.

I turned back to wake Viola. We ran, stumbling, in the darkness to every hermitage, banging on the doors and shouting, "Fire! Fire!" We called 911, but knew it would be a while before any emergency vehicles could make their way to our secluded valley.

I hurried back in the direction of the big building and impulsively rushed inside. It was thick with black smoke. I couldn't see anything and soon felt I was going to pass out. I went back outside for air, then back in, but I was unable to retrieve anything. I did this a few times before giving up entirely.

By now the whole community was there and feeling frantic. I realized our efforts were futile. So I said: "Let it burn. Let it burn. It's not worth anybody getting hurt. Let it burn."

We all walked down to the grove to wait for the fire department. We just kind of stood there, listening to the fire roar, pop, and boom, and we tried to let go of it all.

There came one particularly loud boom, and we began to see dozens—and then hundreds—of what looked like little butterflies hovering around us. They were beautiful embers of light. And we realized that they were paper.

"There goes the library," someone said. "There it goes."

And that's when I felt the loss—thousands of volumes, the repository of so much knowledge and tradition, stored lovingly in bank upon bank of stocked bookshelves.

The "butterflies" flitting around us were pages of Cyprian, Origen, Athanasius, Augustine—my spiritual and intellectual companions as I founded the community. The books, with all my marginal notes, were gone.

———

A fire is a catastrophic loss, and you feel it immediately. Emergency crews worked through the night and overcame the blaze, but it was not long before we began to realize the extent of our losses. Kind neighbors brought us food—but we had no utensils to eat with!

To this day I still begin to walk to the library to retrieve a particular book, only to remember halfway that it isn't there.

Yet I'm also coming to realize that I still have it all. Perhaps my bond with the ancient Fathers is closer than ever.

Early on, when I realized I no longer had my volumes of

the Fathers close at hand, it occurred to me that the Fathers themselves owned very few books. Even for their spiritual descendants in the Middle Ages, books were a rare luxury. There were no printing presses—and certainly no electronic media: no audiobooks, podcasts, software, or websites. Saint Thomas Aquinas once said longingly that he would give all of Paris for just a single volume of Saint John Chrysostom's sermons.

I know that feeling! But I also know that I have what I need of the Fathers. After spending so many years steeped in their lives, I find that their words and ideas arise often in my mind and my prayer. If I have the impulse to reach for their writings, it's because I want to complete a thought already begun. I want to remember where the Fathers went from there.

One of the great lessons I'm still learning from the Fathers is detachment from things, even the best of things—even the beautiful words of the Fathers.

After losing all those thousands of volumes, I'm finding that the witness of the Fathers remains with me, and in many ways it is stronger now than ever. That's the witness I want to share in this book. This book is my "handing on"—that's the literal meaning of the Latin word at the root of *tradition*. We take what our Fathers have given us and pass it along to the next generation.

This book is my retrieval of the companionship of these great men, who have exercised a true fatherhood—a spiritual fatherhood—in my life. I have learned to walk the ancient path because I followed after them, like a little son, watching what they did and trying to learn from them and imitate them.

I think of Saint John Cassian, the great monastic father of the fifth century, and how he spent his youth among the "athletes of prayer" in the Egyptian desert. Later he traveled to France, where he founded monasteries and set down his memories of the great men and women he had met and the lessons they had taught him.

It's my turn now, and I hope you, too, will take your turn. First, before we do our "handing on," we need to receive what the great tradition has carefully kept for us. This book is my act of retrieval and recovery, taking up again what I once received, and sharing the joy of that rediscovery with you, dear friend, as we walk the ancient path together.

There is an enigmatic story preserved in the sayings of the Desert Fathers, from fourth-century Egypt.

> Abba Lot went to see Abba Joseph and said to him: "Abba, as far as I can I say my little office, I fast a little, I pray and meditate, I live in peace as far as I can, I purify my thoughts. What else can I do?" Then the old man stood up and stretched his hands towards heaven. His fingers became like ten lamps of fire and he said to him, "If you will, you can become all flame."[1]

I had consumed all those many books long before the fire consumed them. The last time I saw them, they had indeed "become all flame." Now I need to become what I found in them. I need to become all fire, with a blaze that can consume the world (see Luke 12:49).

Chapter 2

OUR SPIRITUAL FATHERS

I WAS BORN IN 1954 TO A METHODIST MOTHER AND a Presbyterian father. On my mother's side I come from a long line of preachers and circuit riders. My grandfather, James Cochran, was a preacher and a singer, so I've come by my work honestly. He and my grandmother, Maggie, traveled all over western Arkansas and eastern Oklahoma, founding little churches.

I can't say I was raised for the family business. But my parents filled a world with goodness for their three children: my brother, Terry, my sister, Tanni, and me. My childhood days were rich with baseball, music, and the great outdoors. Any one of these pursuits was enough to occupy me through a very happy day. One such day, when I was four, I ventured into the woods on a vacant lot and found a moss-covered "fort" that other children had built and abandoned, probably years before. I spent hours in quiet solitude there while my parents anxiously searched the neighborhood for me.

My parents loved music. When my father was young, he played violin with the local symphony, and Mom played piano. And they recognized that we children had some natural gifts for it. Once, watching television, I saw a man playing banjo, and I was determined to do what he did. I tried to build myself a banjo out of parts I found around the house. My father saw all this and bought me a real one. Then he took a crucial step further. He found me a teacher named Steve Lawrence, who had himself studied under Jerry Waller, who at that time was a banjo player of near-legendary stature where we lived.

My parents, Dick and Jamie, fostered so many natural goods that I still enjoy today. Our religious practice was probably typical of the suburbs in the postwar baby boom. It was regular, though not especially deep. My mother was a pastor's kid, and she had seen the unpleasantness that comes with congregational politics. She was wary of deep engagement. As with many families of our time, religion was something we knew intensely now and then, at Christmas and at funerals.

Even so, God intrudes himself. I remember riding in the car with my dad—I was maybe six years old—and looking out at the nighttime sky. I asked my father, "What is God like?"

He said, "Well, son, he is real big."

Dad accommodated infinity to my six-year-old mind, and I can still meditate on his response today.

My father encouraged all of us children to do what we loved, and, as we grew, music edged out all the other rivals for our attention. He stayed with us. In fact, Dad eventually became our manager and booking agent when my siblings and I launched our professional career in music.

I've rehearsed that career in other books. My friend Dan O'Neill told the story in detail in *Signatures: The Story of John Michael Talbot*. Here it's enough for me to say that our star rose rapidly, first as the Quinchords, then as Sounds Unlimited, then as Mason Proffit, and finally as the Talbot Brothers. We were the advance guard of the "Country Rock" wave that would sweep the country in the 1970s. We experienced all the giddiness of the rise to rock stardom, we played with just about everyone, and we keenly felt the dips in the roller coaster of the music industry. One year John Denver was our opening act. The next year we opened for him! All of this happened quickly and, it seemed, easily. We set our goals, and we achieved them, even while we were still teenagers. I should have been satisfied. Yet I was restless and wanted something more. I looked to the rock stars we were hanging out with, and they had everything we thought we wanted, but they were still unfulfilled and unhappy. I knew there had to be something more.

I began to have questions about God, but I wasn't sure how to pursue them. I looked for transcendence in human love, too, when at seventeen I met Nancy, who was intelligent, beautiful, and three years older. We moved in together, and then, under pressure from my parents, we married and soon had a child.

My religious questions, however, wouldn't go away.

At the beginning of his autobiographical *Confessions,* Saint Augustine wrote: "You have made us for yourself, O Lord, and our hearts are restless until they rest in you." My own story tracks his rather closely at points—and perhaps especially in my twenties. Like Augustine, I was looking for transcendence and ecstasy. Nature presents shadows and images of these in human love, but the heart continues to strive after the divine reality that casts the shadow. If we don't recognize this, we run the risk of making human love into an idol, a false god.

I was in the process of discovering Jesus, and my discovery found a focus of sorts in the Jesus Movement that was then just emerging from the sixties counterculture. As I drew closer to

Jesus, the people around me noticed a change. I was trying to be kind. I was striving not to be the arrogant adolescent I had been.

At the same time I couldn't deny that my relationship with Nancy was faltering. She had married a rising rock star. I was becoming a serious Christian. We were married a few brief years when she confessed to me that she thought we had made a grave mistake. She said that I should have been a monk. In the Jesus Movement at that time, there were many options available, but being a monk wasn't one of them. That's unfortunate, because perhaps I would have benefited if I'd had a sound tradition and community to form me.

More and more I turned inward, but not always in good ways. My mentors in the Jesus Movement encouraged me to memorize Bible verses that could serve as a sure and inflexible rule of life. My "nice guy" phase was short-lived and gave way to a crabbed, closed, judgmental, obsessive phase. I developed opinions about everything. They were usually negative and usually about how other people were living. And I had a Scripture—or three—to back up every opinion. I became insufferable in a new way. My bandmates would probably have preferred my old arrogance to this Christian variety. But I was sure of my rightness.

Inside, however, I was miserable. Nancy and I drifted apart. When we separated, I took refuge with my parents in Indiana, and at their home I proved her right, becoming something of a hermit, craving solitude, spending hours close to nature, trying to pray.

I ventured out in my reading, and I found a kindred spirit in a countercultural wayfarer of another century: Saint Francis of Assisi. I knew there was a Franciscan house nearby, so I made my way there one fine day, and there—while still a "Jesus Freak" and far from Catholicism—I met my spiritual father.

———

The Christian tradition of spiritual fatherhood runs deep. In revealing God to be Father, Jesus relativized human fatherhood. If God himself is the standard for the role, human efforts don't seem to amount to much. "And call no man your father on earth, for you have one Father, who is in heaven" (Matthew 23:9). God's fatherhood is eternal and absolute. He eternally fathers the Son in the Spirit. Before that revelation, all human fatherhood pales almost to insignificance.

I say "*almost* to insignificance," because Saint Paul said that human fatherhood *signifies* God's fatherhood. He said: "For this reason I bow my knees before the Father, from whom all fatherhood in heaven and on earth is named" (Ephesians 3:14-15). The Greek word for "fatherhood" may be, and often is, translated as "family." In the patrilineal culture of Jesus and Paul, the terms were equivalent. Fatherhood and family take their name—they derive their nature—from God's Fatherhood. They are a created, human reflection of God's eternal glory.

So when Jesus relativized fatherhood, he wasn't demoting it or abolishing it. He was calling it to a higher standard, a greater self-giving. No man is father as God is Father. Yet fatherhood itself is divinely designed as a disclosure of God's life.

The inspired Scriptures continued to call men "father." Jesus, in his parables, acknowledged human paternity and used it as a metaphor (see, for example, Luke 15:12). Saint Luke speaks of Joseph as Jesus's "father" (see Luke 2:33), even though Joseph played no biological role in Jesus's conception. Nevertheless, Jesus honored human fatherhood by having an adoptive father. Joseph's fatherhood was far more than mine could ever be, because it was altogether spiritual.

Biblical religion honors fathers, according to the commandment (see Mark 10:19). And the biblical understanding of "fathers" is extensive.[1] It includes all of one's ancestors. *Pateres*—fathers—is the Greek word applied to forebears in the Greek of the New Testament as well as in the Septuagint Greek translation of the Hebrew Old Testament. For Jesus, the "fathers" included the patriarchs of his people and the progenitors in his own bloodline. Luke 1:32 recognizes God's unique fatherhood, even as it applies fatherhood to Jesus's ancestor, the archetypal king of Israel: "He will be great, and will be called the Son of the Most High; and the Lord God will give to him the throne of his father David."

The practice continued in the apostolic Church. John in one passage invokes God's fatherhood and human fatherhood:

I am writing to you, fathers, because you know him who is from the beginning. I am writing to you, young men, because you have overcome the evil one. I write to you, children, because you know the Father. I write to you, fathers, because you know him who is from the beginning. I write to you, young men, because you are strong, and the word of God abides in you, and you have overcome the evil one. (1 John 2:13-14)

Similarly, Stephen applies the term "father" to Abraham (Acts 7:2), and Paul applies it to Isaac (Romans 9:10). Peter refers to the Christians of the first generation as "the fathers" (2 Peter 3:4, where the Greek *pateres* is sometimes translated "ancestors"). And Paul considered himself, as an apostle, to be a father within the Church: "For though you have countless guides in Christ, you do not have many fathers. For I became your father in Christ Jesus through the gospel" (1 Corinthians 4:15).

Again, as in the case of Joseph, Paul is speaking of a fatherhood that is spiritual, not biological, and as such it is a greater fatherhood because it is more like God's own. This is the paternity that the apostles instinctively claimed as their own. In their letters to the churches, they repeatedly address their successors and their congregations as "my child," "my son," and even "little children" (see, for example, Galatians 4:19, 1 Timothy 1:18, Philemon 10, 1 Peter 5:13, 3 John 4).

As it was in the assembly of ancient Israel, so it would be in the assembly that Paul calls the Israel of God, the Church. And so it remains today. We still address our male parents as "Father." We address our priests as "Father." We call the pope "Holy Father." In doing this, we honor Jesus's teaching (Mark 7:10), even as with Saint Paul we recognize God as the source and archetype of all fatherhood. In a similar way, we still call educators "Teacher," though Jesus relativized that title as well (Matthew 23:8). All the great teachers we have on earth are shadows and images of the heavenly teacher.

The Fathers of the Church, like all good fathers, like all good teachers, are icons of God in our lives.

———

From earliest times, Christians have followed the biblical practice of honoring their "fathers"—the ancestors who have gone before them, as well as the "elders" who lead the Church in the current generation. They applied familial terms of endearment to their spiritual authorities. In Egypt and in Rome, they habitually addressed their bishop as *papa*, from which later Christians derived the English title *pope*. The seekers who went out to the desert in search of wisdom called the great ascetics *abba*—that is, *daddy*.

In many cases, people left their family of origin—along with their inheritance—in order to live as children of these spiritual fathers: the bishops of the Church, the ascetics of the desert, the priests in the parish. Christianity had established a new household of God on earth, and its leaders were fathers after the likeness of God.

Every generation sought to follow "the Fathers" in the interpretation of Scripture, in ways of worship, in community discipline, and so on. These things are handed on in the Church, from the fathers in one generation to the children in the next. The Greek word for that "handing on" is *paradosis*; the Latin is *traditio*. What Christ gave to the apostles, the apostles handed on to the Fathers, and the Fathers handed on to us.

The Church, in the Acts of the Apostles, had a developed ritual life, including communal meals, the washing of baptism, and the laying on of hands (Acts 8:18, 9:17). Elsewhere in the New Testament we read of rites for anointing the sick and forgiving sins (James 5:14-16). The Scriptures give limited instructions for these sacraments, or mysteries; rather, they just assume that the rites are already established by custom.

The Fathers preserved the faith of the Church, the ways of scriptural interpretation, and even the canon of Scriptures—guarding this deposit against the corrosive power of heretics, the opposition of pagans, and even the strong tidal force of forgetfulness.

In the early years of the second century, Polycarp of Smyrna, a disciple of the apostle John, declared that "whoever interprets according to his own perverse inclinations, the words of the Lord . . . is the firstborn of Satan."[2] According to Polycarp's disciple Irenaeus of Lyons, the bishop of Smyrna had an opportunity to level the accusation personally at the arch-heretic Marcion, who had denied the authority of the Old Testament. When the two men met on the streets of Rome, Polycarp did not hesitate to call Marcion the devil's spawn.[3]

Scripture was written and compiled by the Church, so it is rightly interpreted in the context of the Church from which and through which it came. To isolate Scripture from its source is to cut it off from the living stream of the Spirit. When we keep it connected to its source we solve many of the modern challenges to the apostolic faith that are really only ancient errors in modern clothes.

—

The ancient tradition—the handing on—describes life as we find it in the Catholic Church, the Orthodox Church, and the other Eastern churches of apostolic origin. The early Protestant reformers sought to follow the pattern as well.

Successive generations of Christians held themselves bound by the practices of the Fathers who had gone before them. It was paramount, then, that they preserve the writings and sayings of the Fathers. Even when the Church was very small—and the faith was illegal and punishable by death—Christians took great care and great risk to have the sermons and letters of the Fathers reproduced by hand. They had no other media at their disposal. And what passed for writing paper in those days was not very durable, so they would usually have to repeat the process every few years.

Yet Christians preserved an impressive number of the works of the Fathers, copying them repeatedly for more than a millennium, till the printing press was used to do the work. We have a handful of works from the first century, more from the second, still more from the third, and many hundreds from the fourth.

Through the second and third centuries, the Church grew large and spread widely. Historians like Hegesippus and Eusebius traveled to visit the archives of individual churches, so that they could conduct research and gather testimonies from the Fathers into more comprehensive books of history. Still later, men like Jerome and Gennadius produced biographies of the Fathers. Though we think of those men as "early Church Fathers," they were already reaching back hundreds of years in their researches.

The testimonies were precious, because they had been preserved at great price and great risk. It was essential that the Church hold itself accountable to the faith as it had been received from the apostles—or, as Saint Vincent of Lérins put it, as it was practiced always, and everywhere, and by everyone.[4]

"Everyone," of course, is a term that must be qualified, because there have always been dissensions in the Church. The Church suffered division and defection even in the days when "the company of those who believed were of one heart and soul" (Acts 4:32). Remember that the primitive community included Ananias and Sapphira, both liars and cheats, who show up just a few verses later. In the book of Revelation, too, we encounter heretics called the Nicolaitans, and the letters of John and Jude refer to still other doctrinal deviations. By the end of the first century, Saint John wrote:

> Many deceivers have gone out into the world, those who do not acknowledge Jesus Christ as coming in the flesh; such is the deceitful one and the antichrist. Look to yourselves that you do not lose what we worked for but may receive a full recompense. Anyone who is so "progressive" as not to remain in the teaching of the Christ does not have God; whoever remains in the teaching has the Father and the Son. (2 John 7-9, NAB)

John is talking about the same sort of men who would later trouble his disciple Polycarp. He is talking about those who would interpret the Gospel in a way different from the way of the Fathers—those who would stray from the ancient path and live a different kind of life and call it "Christian." Heretics have troubled the Church of God in every age.

One hundred percent unanimity has always been a dream of faithful Christians, but it has never been realized, not even in the beginning (at least not for more than a few verses in the Acts of the Apostles!). The measure the Church has always used for fidelity—in doctrine, in interpretation of the Bible, and in ritual practice—is a *consensus* of the Fathers.

———

Fatherhood and tradition are extremely important in biblical religion. Christians and Jews make bold historical claims for their heritage, their patrimony. Our Scriptures testify to events, not

myths. We make our act of faith based on the testimony of reliable witnesses, *eyewitnesses*, whose deeds and words were confirmed by their contemporaries and disciples—whose words and
deeds were, in turn, confirmed by their own cohort. Thus the
Christian family, the Church, has kept its identity and integrity,
as families may, in a chain of memory down the ages.

The ancient rabbis defined a "father" as someone who pre-
cedes us in time and makes us who we are. The definition seems
almost self-evident, but it begs the question: Who *are* we?

"We" are the assembly that the first generation after the
apostles called "the Catholic Church." That is the phrase used
by Ignatius of Antioch, who likely knew Peter, and Polycarp of
Smyrna, who knew John. *Catholic* means "universal," and the
word bespeaks a unity not only in geographic space, but also
in time. The Fathers witness to that unity and serve as its sure
standard.

In those first centuries, the Church grew at an astonish-
ing rate. One modern sociologist estimates that expansion was
steady at 40 percent per decade through the first three centuries of Christian history—centuries of bitter persecution. The
growth was extensive in every direction. The faith spread along
the trade routes by land and sea, conquering individual hearts
first, and then families, and, gradually, peoples.

As the Church grew larger and more ethnically and cultur-
ally diverse, the library of Christian writings grew larger, and it
was apparent that not all of them had the same value.

Which of those authors should be designated as Fathers? In
the fifth century, a monk in Gaul (modern France) addressed
the problem by laying down four criteria for "fatherhood" in the
Church: sanctity, orthodoxy, Church approval, and antiquity.[5]

Sanctity. A Church Father is someone who has not only talked the talk, but also walked the walk. His life expresses his constant desire to do good and avoid evil and to follow Jesus ever more nearly. Such a life manifests God's grace and glory in the world. We say that it is holy. It possesses sanctity. We call such a life the life of a saint.

Orthodoxy. Today we think of this as a name for a particular Christian denomination, the ancient Eastern Churches. Those venerable churches stake their identity on *orthodoxia,* a Greek term that has come to mean "right doctrine." But its deeper meaning is "right praise." The root term *doxos* can denote "praise," and we see it still today in the word *doxology,* which literally means a "word of praise." Orthodoxy requires worship that is in communion and conformity with the apostolic tradition. The Fathers worshipped as the Church worshipped, and lived and died in communion with the Church.

Church approval. Here we see that the designation "Church Father" presumes the existence of the Church. A dad passes on the family identity to the next generation, but it is always an identity he has received. The Church approves the Fathers by citing them as authorities. The teachings of the earliest councils—Nicaea in 325, Constantinople in 381, and Ephesus in 431—turned on questions of scriptural interpretation. The questions were settled as the Church recognized the consensus of those Fathers who were deemed reliable. The Church's definitions went only as far as the Fathers' interpretation would allow.

Antiquity. It's not enough just to be old. At my age I know that to be true. But if a man's teaching endures through centuries, we know that it's not a passing spiritual fad. If successive generations have risked their lives and spent their savings to keep certain books constantly in circulation, we can count that as testimony to the value of those books.

When Anthony the Great was dying, at age 105 in the year 356, he said: "I am going the way of the Fathers . . . for I see myself being summoned by the Lord."

The Church is always going the way of the Fathers, and individually we Christians must walk the ancient path the Fathers blazed for us. Their way is a grace God has given us.

The Fathers of the Church give witness to the Church of the Fathers, and we still live in that Church today. If we confess our sins in a certain way, it is because they have taught us to do so. If we believe, paradoxically, in *both* predestination *and* free will, we do so because they insist that we must. The Fathers keep us from tearing ourselves and our family apart in endless disputes about worship and baptism and beliefs and morals.

The Fathers are true fathers for us, and they exercise a profound spiritual fatherhood.

My father did a beautiful thing when he spoke to me about the bigness of God. The Fathers of the early Church have done so much more.

My father did a beautiful thing for me when he found me a banjo teacher who had himself been instructed by a great master. The Church has done so much more for me in designating certain men to be my spiritual fathers and then preserving their teaching for me.

My experiences of natural fatherhood and musical tradition have been lovely, but my experience of spiritual fatherhood has been far greater. Every earthly fatherhood is partial. Every earthly fatherhood is wounded. Every earthly fatherhood is merely a *shadow* cast by divine reality.

Yet as a shadow cast by a *divine* reality, it also deserves the honor of its name. Though we call no one father as we call God Father, we honor our earthly fathers and mothers, especially those who hold spiritual authority.

Fatherhood is a living thing in any family, but especially in the Church, where God is Father and he exercises his paternity through spiritual leaders and teachers and ministers.

When as a seeker I made my way to that Franciscan house in Indiana, I didn't know that I was walking in the way of the Fathers—and finding a spiritual father. But that's what happened.

Chapter 3

JESUS CHRIST

IKE SO MANY EVANGELICAL CHRISTIANS IN THE 1970s, I came to an awareness of the Church Fathers through the teaching of the great Francis Schaeffer.

An expatriate American, Schaeffer founded a Christian community in Switzerland. He called it L'Abri, Italian for "the shelter." He and his wife, Edith, wrote profoundly influential books advocating a recovery of Christian culture. He engaged social issues, such as abortion, which many Protestant churches and individual believers had long neglected. He was intensely sensitive to beauty in art, music, and literature. When he spoke or wrote, he ranged widely in history. He argued that Western civilization, unmoored from its foundational faith in God, was drifting into decline and decadence.

Yet he was not satisfied simply to observe the culture's crash and burn. He urged Christians to find creative ways to engage the culture. He asked Christian thinkers to retake the ground they had long ago abandoned in philosophy. He called upon artists to live up to their Christian heritage and reflect God's beauty in their creations. He wrote passionate books with provocative titles that dared believers to take a stand: *The Great Evangelical Disaster, How Should We Then Live?*, and *A Christian Manifesto*.

He directed many thousands of Christian followers back to historical sources, especially the Scriptures, but also to the other monuments of Christian culture, including the works of the Church Fathers. As a young musician preoccupied with matters of art and faith, I was drawn to the work and witness of Francis Schaeffer. I pored over his books during those months I spent back at my parents' home in Indiana as my first marriage was ending.

So I was thrilled to hear, on Christian radio, that Schaeffer would soon be lecturing in Indianapolis. He was touring at the time to promote his book *How Should We Then Live?* and he was everywhere drawing great crowds, sometimes numbering in the tens of thousands. It was a curious phenomenon. If you imagine these gatherings to be like Billy Graham Crusades, think again. There was nothing revivalistic about Francis Schaeffer's delivery. He was issuing a summons, but he was delivering it in cold blood. He was lecturing more than preaching. Yet he held his audiences in rapt attention. Whether we were Jesus Freak hippies or button-down members of the emerging suburban superchurches, we were hungry for bread we weren't getting in these American forms of fellowship—in the mainline Protestant churches—and Francis Schaeffer seemed to point to something that would satisfy us.

I was there, of course, in Indianapolis when Schaeffer spoke at the convention center. I was one of six or seven thousand people. It was so incongruous. He sat on a table wearing an alpine Swiss outfit—shorts and high stockings—and casually swinging his legs. He gave a lecture that was more wonky than charismatic. And he was a rock star to that crowd.

At the end of his prepared remarks, he opened the floor to

THE ANCIENT PATH | 45

questions. The first was a big one. Someone asked him what, in his opinion, was the turning point in all history.

By this time we were hanging on his every word. You can imagine the drama, then, when he didn't answer the question immediately. Schaeffer remained silent for probably half a minute—which seemed an eternity in that context.

Then he said: "The Protestant Reformation."

Though I was a Protestant at the time, I felt an immediate, visceral reaction against his answer. I didn't say a word aloud, but my thoughts were clear: *Wrong! No!*

Certainly Francis Schaeffer knew history better than I did. By then, he had been studying it for a long lifetime, in the company of many great minds. I was expert in exactly nothing. But I knew with certainty that he was wrong.

Jesus Christ was, and will always remain, the pivot of history. I didn't know much, but I knew that.

The rest of the session was anticlimactic for me. I was pleased, as I walked into the lobby, to see some other young folks I knew. They asked if I wanted to join them for conversation, and I said sure. I asked where they were staying, and, as if by a providential cue, they said: "Alverna Retreat Center."

It was the Franciscan house near my parents' place.

———

There is a theme that runs through the writings of the Fathers. Many people know it from the Rule of Saint Benedict, but he was quoting it from Saint Cyprian of Carthage, who lived two and a half centuries earlier, dying as a martyr in the middle of the third century.

The theme is simple: *Prefer nothing to Christ.*

If we consider the lives and teachings of the Fathers, we can choose many story lines, and historians have certainly done so. Some tell the story of the early Church as a succession of persecutions. Others trace doctrinal development through controversies and councils. Still others delineate the ways the Church worshipped.

It is simpler, however, and truer to life if we begin with Jesus Christ. He is where the story lines converge.

If Christians were willing to die as martyrs, it was because they wished to imitate Christ and reach Christ. "I am the wheat of God," said Ignatius of Antioch in AD 107. "Let me be ground by the teeth of the wild beasts, that I may be found the pure bread of Christ."[1] Ignatius sought to imitate Jesus not just in dying violently at the hands of the Romans, but in the offering of his body—as "the pure bread of Christ."

If you tell the story of the Church Fathers in terms of doctrinal controversies, once more you must look to Jesus. So many of the Fathers' disputes were with heretics who denied Jesus's humanity or his divinity—or exaggerated one to the seeming exclusion of the other. The Fathers strove to preserve the delicate balance, the precise truth about the incarnation of the Son of God. The early councils were all Christological councils, summoned primarily to settle disputes about the person, natures, and mission of Jesus.

Even the history of the liturgy must proceed by way of Christology, the study of Jesus Christ. For Christ is at the center of the Church's worship. As the first century turned over to the second, even the pagans recognized that Christians worshipped Christ as God.

The early Church preferred nothing—not even life itself—to Christ. The Fathers admirably imitated Saint Paul, who expressed the all-sufficiency of Jesus in various ways. "For I decided to know nothing among you except Jesus Christ, and him crucified" (1 Corinthians 2:2). And "Christ is all and in all" (Colossians 3:11).

Christ, for the Fathers, is at the center of all history. Everything that went before was mere preparation for him; everything afterward is judged by him and in light of him. In the generation after the Apostolic Fathers, Saint Irenaeus said: "the King eternal is raised up, who sums up all things in himself, and has gathered into himself the ancient formation [of man]."[2] Irenaeus, too, follows Saint Paul in speaking of salvation in Christ as a "recapitulation" and climax of all human history. All the blood that had been shed by the Old Testament prophets and righteous ones foreshadowed the atoning blood of Jesus.[3] Christ brought to perfection all that had been prefigured before.

Christ, for the Fathers, was the key to history, the key to true knowledge, the key to heaven.

So they sought Christ in every way he had made himself accessible to them. They pored over Sacred Scripture and sought to draw wisdom from every word. If you page through the multivolume *Ancient Christian Commentary on Scripture*, published by InterVarsity Press, you'll see the depth and breadth of the Fathers' contemplation of the Word of God. The series goes line by line through the Bible, providing the Fathers' interpretations. The collection is vast, and it is still only a small sampling of what has survived the centuries. It is valuable because it brings together the witness of so many authors, geographically and historically dispersed; yet their common instinct was to seek Christ and find him *everywhere* in the sacred texts. "Ignorance of Scripture," said Saint Jerome, "is ignorance of Christ"—and Jerome wrote those words in a book of Old Testament commentary![4]

Nevertheless, Christ was not a *book* for the Fathers. He was a *person*, a *presence*, a *face*. The Fathers, like most Christians throughout most of history, had limited access to the documents of Scripture. Books were a rare commodity—expensive works of scribal art that had to be painstakingly reproduced by hand. The Fathers, as pastors, treasured the books they could acquire, but such acquisitions were limited by their means and circumstances. Still, they had Christ. "For where two or three are gathered in my name," Jesus said, "there am I in the midst of them" (Matthew 18:20). The Fathers took the Lord at his word. In the prayer and ministry of the Church, they experienced his nearness and his friendship. Jesus was proclaimed in the Scriptures and revealed to them in the breaking of the bread, just as he had been for the disciples at Emmaus (Luke 24:35).

Again, he was not a book, but rather a *fact*, a reality. He was historical, but not simply past. He was awaited and expected, but not relegated to a point in the near or distant future. He was ever present, experienced mystically and spiritually. "Jesus Christ is the same yesterday and today and for ever" (Hebrews 13:8). And he was relevant to everything in creation.

Given the dearth of written Scripture texts, you'd think that it would be easy for Jesus to become a Rorschach blot for far-flung Christians, a vague concept they could interpret as they wished—or a projection of their own presuppositions, their fondest wishes, or their prejudices. You'd think that there would be a diversity of "Jesuses" on offer in the world of the early Christians, but there were not.

Already in the generation after the apostles, the Fathers spoke of a "Catholic Church,"[5] a unified, universal body that professed a common faith in Jesus Christ. There was nothing iffy about their profession. Ignatius of Antioch, who had learned his doctrine from the apostles, repeatedly spoke of "Jesus Christ our God."[6] He spoke also of Jesus's true humanity in the flesh— flesh that was descended from the Old Testament King David[7] and really suffered on the cross.[8] He insisted, moreover, that that Jesus's same human flesh became the "bread of God"[9] and was consumed in the Eucharist.[10] Thus, orthodox faith in Jesus Christ led to identifiably correct Christian practice. For Ignatius, the mark of heresy was to deny the true humanity of Jesus and his presence in the Eucharist.[11]

It is remarkable that even the persecutors got their Christology right. Around the year AD 112, the proconsul of Bithynia, Pliny the Younger, wrote a report to the emperor Trajan outlining Christian beliefs as well as he could determine them (by interrogating Christians under torture). His details are sketchy, but he describes what is clearly a Sunday gathering for the Eucharist, where food of a harmless sort is consumed and where the people sing "hymns to Christ as to a god."[12]

From the first generation, Christians were those who believed in the true deity of Christ and in his true incarnation—his enfleshment—his humanity. The Christian faith was clear and identifiable, though it wasn't exactly propositional or precisely formulated till later centuries. Even in the first generations, even a pagan like Pliny could sort it out.

The apostles themselves faced challenges from "deceivers" who denied Jesus's humanity (see 2 John 1:7), and they did not hesitate to declare such men accursed. Ignatius of Antioch recognized the same boundaries when he condemned the bad faith of the "Docetists," so named because they taught that Jesus only "seemed" to be human (in Greek, "to seem" is *dokeo*).

The doctrine of the earliest Fathers was inchoate. There were challenges still to come, and those challenges would force doctrinal development. The Fathers did not—and could not—change the Church's traditional faith regarding Jesus Christ. They would, however, need to refine their expressions of that faith, as theological speculation grew ever more subtle. Would it be possible, for example, to affirm that Jesus was "divine" without saying he was coeternal with God? In the fourth century, Arius posed that question and gathered many followers after him, including some emperors and bishops. The Councils of Nicaea (AD 325) and Constantinople (381) were convoked to consider a cluster of questions related to Jesus's deity, and in between the councils the apostolic faith was articulated by great men such as Athanasius of Alexandria and the Cappadocian Fathers: Basil the Great, Gregory of Nazianzus, and Gregory of Nyssa.

The Church Fathers developed a formula in the fourth century, but there was nothing novel about it. It was consistent with earlier creeds (like the Apostle's Creed) and the even earlier testimonies of apostolic men like Ignatius and Polycarp. The children of the Fathers use those ancient words even today to profess the classic faith in Jesus Christ. The Nicene-

Constantinopolitan Creed is a staple of Sunday worship in many liturgical churches:

I believe in one Lord Jesus Christ,
the Only Begotten Son of God,
born of the Father before all ages.
God from God, Light from Light,
true God from true God,
begotten, not made, consubstantial
with the Father;
Through him all things were made.

Christians who hold themselves accountable to these words are likely to hold fast to the biblical faith—the faith that the apostles received from Jesus and then passed on within the Church. Christians who recite the ancient creeds with conviction will indeed *prefer nothing to Christ*—the God-Man whom they truly know! They will prefer nothing to Christ, though they, like Athanasius, should suffer exile and lose their jobs—though they, like Ignatius and Polycarp, should face the threat of torture and death.

"Prefer nothing to Christ," said Saint Cyprian, "because he preferred nothing to us, and on our account preferred hard things to ease, poverty to riches, servitude to rule, death to immortality."[13]

⸺

If Christ is preferable to everything on earth, he must be better than everything on earth. We naturally prefer what is better to what is worse. So if we are to prefer hard things—like poverty, servitude, and death—for Christ's sake, it is because Christ is worth the trouble. He has re-ordered all human values, because he is divine.

Jesus's divinity is assumed everywhere in the New Testament. The evangelist speaks of him as the eternal Word who was always with God and "was God" (John 1:1). Jesus himself tells of his union with God, whom he calls "Father" (John 10:38). Doubting Thomas addresses Jesus as "My Lord and my God!" (John 20:28). Saint Paul describes Jesus as living "in the form of God" (Philippians 2:6). And the Epistle to the Hebrews identifies Jesus in terms that should only be applied to God: "He reflects the glory of God and bears the very stamp of his nature, upholding the universe by his word of power. When he had made purification for sins, he sat down at the right hand of the Majesty on high" (Hebrews 1:3).

Jesus is God, yet he is distinct from his Father, who is also God. The Lord speaks, too, of a Paraclete, or Advocate, a Consoler and Counselor, the Holy Spirit, who is equally divine (John 14:26). This Paraclete descended on the Church with power, as the gift of the Father and the Son, on the first Christian Pentecost (see Acts 2).

Jesus is God, and still he lives in communion with two other divine persons. And yet Christian witness is unanimous in the profession that "God is one" (see Romans 3:30, Galatians 3:20, James 2:19). Even Saint Paul acknowledged the mysterious nature of Jesus's revelation. How can God be simultaneously "one" and "more than one" (Galatians 3:20)?

Jesus told us things we could never figure out with our own brain power. He arrived as God's perfect self-revelation. Encountering Jesus, the apostles encountered also the Father and the Spirit—because the divine persons are inseparable.

> Philip said to him, "Lord, show us the Father, and we shall be satisfied."
> Jesus said to him, "Have I been with you so long, and yet you do not know me, Philip? He who has seen me has seen the Father; how can you say, 'Show us the Father'?" (John 14:8-9)

Jesus revealed God to be a Trinity of persons. Thus, Jesus revealed God to be love. The God of Jesus Christ is not just a lover, and not just loving. God is love (1 John 4:8, 16). God is himself an eternal act of loving communion: "The grace of the Lord Jesus Christ and the love of God and the fellowship of the Holy Spirit be with you all" (2 Corinthians 13:14).

We could not know this unless it had been revealed in a powerful, personal way. Jesus is that revelation. He is everything that God has to say about himself. Here's how the early Church Father Tertullian put it: "The expression 'God the Father' had never been revealed to anyone. When Moses himself asked God who he was, he heard another name. The Father's name has been revealed to us in the Son, for the name 'Son' implies the new name 'Father.'"[14]

Jesus is not a book. He is a divine person, come to reveal the mysterious nature of divinity—God's inner life, which would be otherwise unknowable to us. Jesus communicated that life to us not merely in prose, or poetry, or myth, or epics, but rather in himself—in humanity, in flesh. He gave himself, in flesh and blood, to the Church. He did not write a book, but gathered a people, from whom he chose identifiable leaders to serve as authorities when he returned to heaven. He then sent the Spirit to empower us.

He established the Church to be his body on earth. The apostles taught the world with their living voices. The Scriptures are the earliest written record of apostolic teaching, and so they became the *kanon*—the measuring stick, the canon—by which all other teaching is measured. The Scriptures are part and parcel of Jesus's self-revelation; they participate in that revelation, but they themselves are not the limits of revelation. Indeed, in the Acts of the Apostles, we see revelation spread through Asia Minor and into Europe, years before the inspired words were set down on parchment. Thus the Scriptures reflect a Church already in existence—a sacramental Church with a developed ritual life and theology.

Jesus made this possible. To know him was, and is, in some sense to know the mystery of God.

How do the Fathers figure in this exchange? The Dominican theologian Aidan Nichols, building on the work of Joseph Ratzinger (later Pope Benedict XVI), argued that the Fathers "have a constitutive role in Christian faith because their response to Scripture was a constitutive element in the happening of the Word of God in revelation."[15]

Revelation, Father Nichols explains, is *communication*. God speaks to us. But it's not enough simply to disclose information. A disclosure is not truly revelation unless it's *received:* "one cannot speak of revelation strictly so called unless one assumes that revelation has really been received." Communication is a two-way process. It requires a speaker and a listener, a writer and a reader, a messenger and a recipient. Revelation communicates God's inner life, but it is the task of humankind to receive it and freely accept it.

Nichols, again following Ratzinger, argues that "the 'moment' of the Fathers was an essential moment in the receiving of the Word of God by the Church." The work of the Fathers was the Church's great "Amen!" to all that God had revealed in Jesus Christ.

What, then, did the Fathers do? They set the limits of the Christian biblical canon, they crafted the classic creeds, they laid down the methods of scriptural interpretation, and they established the Church's moral discipline and sacramental rites. These works are constitutive of Christian faith. We need the closed biblical canon, for example, as a clear boundary line, and the Fathers laid it down for us in the late fourth century. The revelation had taken place long before, but the *Amen* resounded from the Church—and for the Church—in the work of the Fathers, such as Athanasius, Augustine, and Damasus.

The work of these men was nothing more than an Amen to Jesus, whom they knew as the Lord of history and the Lord of their lives. Jesus was the agenda of their councils, the refrain in their hymns, the figure at the center of their icons.

If we know Jesus today as Lord of history and Lord of our lives, it is because of the role the Fathers played in receiving God's definitive self-revelation—the special role that was assigned to them by God.

Not every teacher is a "father." The apostle Paul made that clear: "For though you have countless guides in Christ, you do not have many fathers" (1 Corinthians 4:15). So it is probably unfair for me to juxtapose Francis Schaeffer's spontaneous comment with the carefully collated, edited, and translated thoughts of the early Fathers of the Church.

I've done this, however, not to dismiss Francis Schaeffer or diminish him. He was (and he remains) profoundly influential in my life and in the lives of millions of others. Yet, for me, he pointed beyond himself to greater teachers who were more than teachers—teachers who were, like Paul, also fathers. It was Francis Schaeffer who made me go deep in history, and, like John Henry Newman, I concluded that "to be deep in history is to cease to be a Protestant."[16]

Francis Schaeffer was, in my opinion, the most articulate opponent of the trendy existentialism that was so common among the countercultural movements of the 1960s. It may have had its origins in the postwar philosophy of Jean-Paul Sartre and Albert Camus, but by the time of my young adulthood its most effective medium was the lyrics of popular music. From the clubs of Liverpool to the street corners of Haight-Ashbury, the basic principle was the same: truth was a pure, deeply felt subjective experience, beyond objective revelation or verification. My generation was all about forcing open the gates of mystery, by whatever means: cannabis, LSD, TM, or the *Kama Sutra*. It was an oddly united cultural force, bringing together a motley assortment of young people whose only creed was the rejection of the old authorities.

Against this cultural tide, Schaeffer boldly proposed divine revelation that was objective and absolute. He presented intelligent and persuasive arguments for the inspiration and inerrancy of Scripture. That's what grabbed me at first.

It failed me, eventually, because it seemed to lead back to the same strange existentialism I saw everywhere else. Schaeffer wanted us to take an existential leap and believe Scripture without understanding the divinely established authority that gave us the Scriptures.

For me, faith had to be more than a leap into the dark. As I studied the origins of Scripture, I found myself confronted by the earthly authority that preceded, produced, confirmed, conserved, and canonized the books of the Bible.

So it was Schaeffer's search for objective truth that led me to the primacy of Jesus. But I came to conclude that Schaeffer ended his journey short of the destination. He raised the question about existentialism but failed to answer it. Still, his questions set me on the path on which I eventually encountered the Fathers of the Church.

It was Francis Schaeffer's "wrong" answer that made me consider, as never before, the centrality of Jesus in my own life and in human history and culture.

It was Francis Schaeffer's lecture that occasioned my visit to the house of another Francis—Saint Francis of Assisi—and it was there that I met the man who would become my first spiritual father.

For all of that, I am deeply grateful to Francis Schaeffer.

———

After the conclusion of Schaeffer's talk, I left the Convention Center with some friends who were staying at the Alverna Retreat Center (because they couldn't afford a hotel room).

I was preoccupied by Schaeffer's answer, and I said so. We were a mixed group, denominationally speaking, which made for a lively discussion. One of the resident friars, Father Martin Wolter, joined us. Soon we moved from the rightness or wrongness of the speaker to the general principle.

Father Martin seemed to understand my hang-up, and he had an interesting take on the matter.

Everything before Christ, he said, funnels down to Jesus—everything: all the philosophers, all the world religions, the prophets and patriarchs of Israel, all of it goes—*bang!*—inexorably into Christ. Christ recapitulates it all, corrects it, and perfects it. The hopes and fears of all the years are met in Jesus at the moment of his incarnation. And that's true, too, Father Martin explained, of everything that came after Christ.

The man spoke with a simple wisdom. Much later I would recognize his ideas as I encountered them in Saint Irenaeus and Saint Paul, but that evening I was impressed by the way they came readily to his lips, as if they were as obvious to him as the old paneling on the friary walls.

I was drawn to the naturalness of his faith. It seemed total, but not in the wild-eyed, obsessed way of a Flannery O'Connor street prophet. His manner was self-effacing and free of any drama.

I knew then—again, before I was Catholic—that he would be my spiritual father. What made it clear to me was not, I insist, confirmation bias. I was happy that this wise man agreed with me. But I was more impressed by what separated him from me: his serenity, his rest in God, and his joyful, humble confidence in a truth that was bigger than he was, bigger than any denomination or historical movement—a truth he didn't have to invent, but only receive.

Father Martin wasn't a spiritual father from central casting.

He loved a cold beer and a hearty laugh. He could be as aggravating as he was charming. There was nothing stereotypically sanctimonious about him, and in that, as in many other qualities, he was like the early Church Fathers. There was nothing Hollywood saintly about Saint Jerome; he was famous for grumpiness even in his own lifetime. There was nothing saccharine about Saint Cyril of Alexandria, who was a first-rate political operator in the rough-and-ready fifth century. Dads come in more varieties than Heinz pickles. Yet God calls every sort of person to share in Jesus's holiness and apostolate.

In many ways, Father Martin was an ordinary Catholic. He manifested no unusual gifts or prodigies. He showed what a run-of-the-mill guy could become by the habit of fidelity to the Church of Jesus Christ. As an ordinary Catholic—receiving the sacraments and discerning his particular vocation—he had walked the ancient path, the way of the Fathers. And simply by fidelity to the Church's way he had shared the Fathers' great Amen, their "yes" to God's self-revelation in Jesus. He was at home in the household they had built. The creeds and councils, the dogmas and liturgies were like the walls of a home, at once protective and comforting—so familiar as to be unremarkable.

In time I told him I wanted him to be my spiritual father. In his laid-back, good-natured way he accepted. He preferred to be more of a companion to me, but I made it clear that I would consider him to be speaking with authority. In my intense and deliberate way I told him in no uncertain terms that I was serious about the request. If I was going to call him "Father," then he was going to be a daddy to me, and he would possess authority I would be bound in conscience to recognize. At the time, I wasn't Catholic, but I understood the fatherhood Saint Paul had exercised in the Corinthian church. I was asking Father Martin to be the same kind of father to me. He accepted the terms.

Years later I am still striving to understand the nature of the role of spiritual father, which I now hold for others. (I long to be as effective with them as Father Martin was with me.) I am forever grateful that Father Martin accepted me in my youthful zeal and gave me an example I still learn from, even after his death and passing to the Lord.

When we call the great men of the early Church "fathers," we are acknowledging the authority they have in God's household, and we are binding ourselves to their word and witness. We are accepting them and their fundamental plan for our lives: that we should prefer nothing—nothing!—to Jesus Christ.

Chapter 4

SALVATION

OVER WEEKS AND MONTHS I BECAME PART OF the Alverna family, a familiar face on the grounds, at table, and in the halls. As I came to know Father Martin, I began to see how he was formed by a particular tradition I could trace back to Saint Francis of Assisi. As I read about Saint Francis, I began to see how he was himself formed by a tradition I could trace back to the Desert Fathers of Egypt in the third and fourth centuries—ascetics who gave up riches to find solitude with the Lord. And then I could see that they, too, were part of a tradition that went back to John the Baptist—as John, in turn, was part of a tradition that stretched back through the Old Testament prophets to the very waters of creation.

It was Alverna's functional family life that enabled me to see how tradition forms a home. The common life at the retreat house was not ideal—what family home is?—but it worked. It was functional, despite some inevitably dysfunctional members, and it helped me to begin to understand the Church as a family.

I began to see that Protestant Christianity also had its own traditions—its own patterns of family life. We Protestants had our Sinner's Prayer and altar calls, our interpretive methods and interpretive taboos. We also had our many and varied "Orders of Worship" and liturgies. They were patterns of family life I could trace back to a certain period in history. They had been handed on by one generation to the next. They could not be found explicitly in Scripture, but I could see how they grew out of a certain way of reading Scripture—a tradition preserved in an institution, a church.

My explorations gradually led me to intensive study of the earliest Christian documents outside the Scriptures—the writings of the men we call the Apostolic Fathers. I pored over these, as I wanted to see the Church in its primitive purity. I wanted to see how the disciples of the apostles lived the teachings I found in the Acts of the Apostles. Clement of Rome, after all, had sat at the feet of Peter and Paul. Ignatius had succeeded Peter as bishop of Antioch. Polycarp had received the faith from John. The *Didache*—which almost certainly contained the earliest records of all—was presented as the "The Doctrine of the Lord, Through the Twelve Apostles, to the Nations." That's the literal translation of its Greek title.

I inclined toward these earliest authors because their simplicity reminded me of Scripture. I had been led, moreover, to distrust the documents of a later age. Historians in the tradition of the Protestant Reformation often draw a sharp distinction between the pre- and post-Constantinian periods. It all turned on the fourth century. Constantine, they said, ruined the Church, or at least tainted it, by institutionalizing it and making it more congenial to pagans, adopting the practices of mystery religions, imposing a hierarchical structure, and so on.

What I found, however, in those early documents was a people who identified as a Church—in Greek, *ekklesia*, assembly. And that assembly had an identifiable hierarchical form, and that assembly celebrated *mysteria,* or "mysteries," the Greek term we Westerners translate as "sacraments." The Church was a "body," with a heart for devotion, a head for doctrinal direction, and a structure for unified functionality. These were primitive and developing, but the essentials were clearly in place from the earliest years and decades.

All this was true, of course, even with the descent of the Holy Spirit at Pentecost (Acts 2). Commentators today sometimes treat the Spirit's gifts, or charisms, as if they're somehow *opposed* to the Church's institutions and offices. But it's clear from the Scriptures that the offices and the institution were public and identifiable on the same day the charisms appeared. These were not opposed, but rather were complementary of each other, and often both were present in one person who was in leadership. Many people experienced a conversion on Pentecost. Many people heard the proclamation and understood it. Many people repented of their sins. But in that great crowd of men and women, only the apostles spoke and acted with authority, and pre-eminent among the apostles was Peter.

The work of the Church was salvation—bringing the Good News of Jesus Christ to the whole world—saving people from their sins. And that was still good news to me. I had long ago put off the destructive habits of a rock-and-roll lifestyle. Now my experience of sin was tangled up in the scandal of confusion in Christianity itself: the conflicting interpretations of Scripture and the sometimes fierce and mutually destructive divisions perpetuated by believers. As much as I needed salvation from my old sins, I also needed to be saved from the mess of contemporary Christianity.

The Church, in fact, was the ordinary means of salvation,

established by Jesus, and it applied salvation by means of the sacramental mysteries, also established by Jesus. Three thousand were baptized on Pentecost (Acts 2:41), and their life afterward was centered on the Eucharist: "the apostles' teaching and fellowship, to the breaking of bread and the prayers" (Acts 2:42).

That is the same Church I encountered in the works of the Apostolic Fathers. They shared Saint Peter's conviction that "baptism . . . now saves you" (1 Peter 3:21) and Saint Paul's belief in the Eucharist as a communion in the Body and Blood of Jesus (1 Corinthians 10:16-17). I encountered the ideal harmony between personal salvation and reception of the sacraments as a Spirit-filled, life-giving personal encounter with Jesus Christ.

Consider the *Didache*.

The *Didache* is a manual of Church order—a kind of instruction book on how to run a Christian community. Scholars believe that it emerged from Syrian Antioch, the city where the disciples were first called "Christians" and the home of the first-century bishop who first used the term "Catholic Church." Though the text may have reached its final form in the early second century, the *Didache's* ritual portions seem to have been set in writing much earlier. These may have been composed before the Council of Jerusalem, which is described in chapter 15 of the Acts of the Apostles.[1]

The *Didache* begins by contrasting two possible "ways" to live life on earth: the way of life and the way of death. Subsequent chapters sketch out, in very specific and practical terms, the moral actions that characterize each "way." The *Didache* condemns abortion, for example, in the strongest terms, as "murder." It forbids employers any actions that would scandalize the faith of their employees. The *Didache,* it seemed to me, had the ring of authenticity, issuing a call to radical discipleship. It applied the principles of the Sermon on the Mount in nitty-gritty ways to daily life. My heart leapt as I read how the early Christians actually lived their faith. What I was looking for in the works of various reformers and movements I was finding here, in this most ancient text. This had a powerful moral effect on me, making me want to go and do the same.

Yet it's not all about morals. Arguably, it's not *primarily* about morals. It's about relationship with Jesus—relationship in a way that unites his followers in tangible ways: in lifestyle, leadership, and worship. Christian morality flows from that relationship with Jesus, leads us back to him, and causes that relationship to grow stronger through real personal and communal holiness.

The *Didache* presents the moral life—made up of our everyday actions and choices—as a preparation for mystical and sacramental life. The great concern of the *Didache* is the Church's ritual public worship, its liturgy; all other concerns are examined in light of proper worship. Divine worship is what unites us to Jesus and with one another.

In this way, the *Didache* follows the same line of argument as chapters 10 and 11 in Saint Paul's First Epistle to the Corinthians:

> Whoever, therefore, eats the bread or drinks the cup of the Lord in an unworthy manner will be guilty of profaning the body and blood of the Lord. Let a man examine himself, and so eat of the bread and drink of the cup. For any one

who eats and drinks without discerning the body eats and drinks judgment upon himself. (1 Corinthians 11:27-29)

The *Didache*, in its central chapters, chapters 6–16, focuses primarily on the right and wrong ways to observe the sacraments of the Church, above all baptism and the Eucharist, but also penance (the confession of sins) and holy orders (sacred ministry).

Baptism, according to the instruction, must be conducted with the trinitarian formula, as Jesus commanded (see Matthew 28:19). But the *Didache* acknowledges several options for the rite of baptism. The preferred way is by immersion in cold, running ("living") water, but stagnant water will do when running water is unavailable, and warm water will do in the absence of cold. In a pinch, says the *Didache*, the Church is free to baptize by pouring water over the new Christian—three times, in the name of the Father, and of the Son, and of the Holy Spirit.

Here the basic essentials of the faith were already in place, but not so much as propositions or institutions, but rather as a God-given means of receiving and maintaining the grace of a personal relationship with Jesus Christ. The grace was at once individual and communal. That relationship and that communion were the key to understanding everything else about the early Church.

In the *Didache*, there is a sense of reality and gravity about the Church's worship. The sacrament is something important, something that demands serious preparation. The *Didache* counsels both the baptizer and the baptized to fast for days before the administration of the rite! The *Didache* enjoins the whole Church, in fact, to lead a rigorous ascetical life, fasting twice a week (Wednesday and Friday) and praying three times a day.

For those who have sinned the way is clear: "In the church you shall confess your sins, and you shall not come near for your prayer with an evil conscience. This is the way of life" (*Didache* 4). Confession before Communion was the norm, according to chapter 14 of that work: "But every Lord's Day gather yourselves together, and break bread, and give thanksgiving after having confessed your sins, that your sacrifice may be pure" (*Didache* 14).

We see that worship of the early Church took place on Sundays. We see that the Eucharist was considered a "sacrifice." We find out in chapter 9 of the *Didache* how the offering was to take place. In the same passage we learn that the first Christians also practiced closed Communion, admitting only believers. And we find echoes, too, of the Pauline teaching that the Eucharist is the source and sign of the Church's unity (compare 1 Corinthians 10:17 and *Didache* 9).

The *Didache* presents salvation not as the matter of a moment, but as a way of life. It is a life lived in the Church—a life born from the baptismal waters and fed at the Lord's table. The Church sustains God's children and strengthens them for life on earth, which—make no mistake—is a trial. "But those who endure in their faith shall be saved from under the curse itself" (*Didache* 16).

The ordinary means of salvation are the Church itself and the sacraments that Jesus has entrusted to the Church. Salvation is personal, but not simply individualistic. Everything about it has a communal dimension as well.

I read the *Didache* in the woods around Alverna. From there I went on to Pope Saint Clement's *Letter to the Corinthians;* another letter commonly attributed to Barnabas, the companion of Saint Paul; the seven letters of Saint Ignatius of Antioch; and the letter of Saint Polycarp to the Philippians. Beyond that first sub-apostolic generation, I read the great apologists, Justin and Aristides and Athenagoras. I read the great Africans Tertullian and Perpetua.

I found, to my surprise, that their most urgent common concern was not so much "theology" as worship—sacramental worship—the mysteries of the Church. For love is a mystery, explainable and guided in part by truth, but beyond full description. Everything flowed from that personal, loving relationship with Jesus, and communion with one another in Jesus. Later concerns about speculative matters were not yet on their radar. They were intensely concerned about salvation, and to be saved meant to be in the Church of Jesus Christ, the ark of salvation. The Church of Jesus Christ was, for them, the home of the saved, the shelter of the saved, and the family of the saved. Belonging to the Church, worshipping with the Church, was, for them, the condition of being saved.

Through baptism those early Christians had been born into the family, into a new way of living. The waters made a difference. In the first-century Epistle of Barnabas we read: "we descend into the water full of sins and defilement, and we come up bearing fruit in our hearts, fear [of the Lord] and trust in Jesus in the Spirit."[2] Thus, the waters were an essential beginning to new life in Christ. Tertullian wrote: "No one can attain salvation without baptism. The Lord said: Unless one is born of water, he cannot enter into the kingdom of heaven"[3] (see John 3:5).

The Eucharist was, for the earliest Church Fathers, "the medicine of immortality."[4] It was the only true antidote to death. It was Jesus's own sacrifice, sacramentally extended and given to the Church. It was the true celebration of the Lord's Day. It was the flesh of Christ, the blood of God.

None of this was a late development. It was not an invention of the Constantinian church. It was the most primitive faith. You and I could fill a book simply by walking through Clement, Ignatius, Polycarp, and Barnabas and drawing out the sacramental teachings as we did for the *Didache*. We need not enter the third century in order to see the consistency—indeed, the unanimity—of the Fathers' testimony. The Fathers lived in a sacramental Church, the Church they had received in trust from the apostles, who received it in trust from Jesus. This became clear to me as I meditated, alone with my books, in the forest.

Reading those most ancient texts, I was inspired to begin composing the songs that made up my album *The Lord's Supper*. I wanted nothing more than to echo the song of salvation as I found it in the books of the New Testament and the writings of the early Church Fathers.

In the twentieth century, the novelist Flannery O'Connor said of the Eucharist, "Well, if it's a symbol, to hell with it."[5] Like the Fathers of the first and second centuries, she was impressed with the flesh-and-blood realism of Jesus's promise in the Bread of Life Discourse (John 6:26-69). Jesus was not waxing poetic. The more the people were repulsed by his exhortation to eat his flesh and drink his blood, the more he sharpened his language. By the end of that chapter of the Gospel, it's clear that no one was using or taking the terms in a metaphorical way—not Jesus, not the apostles, and not the ex-disciples who walked away in disgust and disbelief.

Why was Jesus so insistent? Because he was talking about the means and the meaning of his saving work. "I came that they may have life, and have it abundantly" (John 10:10). It is through the sacraments, particularly baptism and Eucharist, that he gives this life. Though Jesus's interlocutors knew the Scriptures, they were not getting his message: "You search the scriptures, because you think that in them you have eternal life; and it is they that bear witness to me; yet you refuse to come to me that you may have life" (John 5:39-40).

Only God possesses true life, *divine life,* by nature, "in himself" (John 5:26). Yet "God so loved the world that he gave his only Son, that whoever believes in him should not perish but have eternal life" (John 3:16). To possess this life is to share in God's very nature (see 2 Peter 1:4). To live such a life requires a human being to undergo a new birth, to be strengthened by a new form of sustenance. We must begin to live as God lives.

This is a recurrent theme in the fourth Gospel, and it echoes often in the early Fathers. Jesus gives "the food which endures to eternal life" (John 6:27), the bread that "gives life to the world" (6:33), the "Bread of Life" that is Jesus himself. Those who believe in him shall "have eternal life" (6:40), something that belongs only to God. If we receive the Eucharist, we can be assured of our resurrection (6:54). Unless we receive it, we have "no life" in us (6:53).

Ah, here again are those "two ways" we encountered in the *Didache*—the way of life and the way of death (which is "no life").

There is a birth and there is a sustenance that are proper to the Way of Life, and these are the ordinary means by which God applies salvation to sinners. These are the sacraments of divine life. There are good Gospel reasons that the *Didache* places such strong emphasis on the sacraments.

We cannot receive God's full and abundant life unless we are first transformed. A vessel has to be prepared for what it will contain, or it will lose what it has received. A clay jar must be fired in a kiln and ready for water, or it will spill the water and come apart in the process. To receive divine life unprepared would be like receiving the hottest fire. We, as sinners, could never endure contact with an all-holy God. Only God can endure contact with God. That is why he came to save us as he did: to share his life and make us a new creation. We must, he said, become once again like little children and even be born again. Rather than live in our usual human element, we must come to live "in Christ," the eternal Son of God (Romans 6:11), so that he will come to live in us (Colossians 1:27). Thus we may begin to live as children of God. Both the preparing and the filling are gifts of grace.

This is salvation. Jesus came to "save his people from their sins" (Matthew 1:21). But there is so much more to the story! He came so that we might have *life*—his life, divine life—and have it abundantly. That's salvation. That's heaven. That's what Jesus gave us in his human life. That's what he still gives us in his sacraments.

—

Salvation is not just about praying a Sinner's Prayer and reading the Bible. It is a radical, but not fanatical, change of our entire life. It is a "graced exchange." The Son of God left eternity for time, and he calls us to leave the things of time for the things of eternity. It saves us and changes us completely for the better.

In his compact summary of salvation history, Saint Paul spoke of this exchange:

> But when the time had fully come, God sent forth his Son, born of woman, born under the law, to redeem those who were under the law, so that we might receive adoption as sons. And because you are sons, God has sent the Spirit of his Son into our hearts, crying, "Abba! Father!" So through God you are no longer a slave but a son, and if a son then an heir. (Galatians 4:4-7)

"For you know the grace of our Lord Jesus Christ, that though he was rich, yet for your sake he became poor, so that by his poverty you might become rich" (2 Corinthians 8:9).

The classic question of theology is Why did God become man? Well, there's the answer. "For your sake"! "So that . . . you might become rich"!

We are saved from our sins, but we are saved to become God's children. Through baptism, we come to share the nature of the Son because he first came to share our nature. Saint Irenaeus put it poetically: In the incarnation, the Holy Spirit "grew accustomed" to living in human flesh.[6]

In baptism and Eucharist, we know true communion with God in all his glory—though we do not yet see that glory. In our flesh and blood, we are united with God's flesh and blood. In our spirit, we know union with his Spirit. The same bond of love that binds the Trinity binds us in Jesus Christ.

For all who are led by the Spirit of God are sons of God. For you did not receive the spirit of slavery to fall back into fear, but you have received the spirit of sonship. When we cry, "Abba! Father!" it is the Spirit himself bearing witness with our spirit that we are children of God, and if children, then heirs, heirs of God and fellow heirs with Christ, provided we suffer with him in order that we may also be glorified with him. (Romans 8:14-17)

Divine life is ours for the living—if we accept it and persevere in it. It is ours, "provided we suffer with" Jesus Christ. That, surely, is the trial we hear about at the end of the *Didache*—the trial that is an unavoidable part of life on earth—the trial for which we are strengthened by the life of the Church, especially in the sacraments.

By ourselves, we cannot prevail over suffering and death. That is why God empowers us to live a human life by his divine strength. We live the life of Christ. We imitate Christ. We suffer with Christ. So great is our dignity now that God empowers us to *"[complete] what is lacking in Christ's afflictions* for the sake of his body, that is, the church" (Colossians 1:24).

We suffer with Christ. We suffer in Christ. We suffer as the Body of Christ. Even as we suffer—especially as we suffer—we are living the life of the God-Man. We are divinized, deified, and glorified as God's children.

Saint John sounds astonished as he writes about this dimension of our salvation: "See what love the Father has given us, that we should be called children of God; and so we are" (1 John 3:1).

So we are! We, too, should be astonished.

The Eastern Fathers spoke of the graced exchange in Greek terms that are startling to Western ears. They called it *theopoiesis*—literally, "god-making." They called it *theosis*—which can be translated, roughly, as *godding*.[7] In saving us, God has "godded" us by making us partakers of his divine nature (2 Peter 1:4).

Saint Irenaeus, in the second century, gave us a classic formula of the doctrine of deification: "For this reason the Word of God was made man, and he who was the Son of God became the Son of Man: so that man, now taken into the Word and receiving adoption, might become the son of God."[8] Later in the same work, the bishop said: "We follow the only true and steadfast teacher, the Word of God, our Lord Jesus Christ, who, through his transcendent love, became what we are so that he might bring us to be what he is himself."[9]

Saint Athanasius of Alexandria, in the fourth century, said it most concisely: "He was made man that we might be made God."[10] This does not mean we're given permission to walk around acting like we're God Almighty. No, it is a divine gift that makes us even more perfectly human.

God gave us divinity. We gave him humanity. The Son of God became the Son of Man so that the sons and daughters of men might become the sons and daughters of God. You'll find the same thought expressed in varied and beautiful forms in the writings of many of the Fathers: Saint Gregory of Nazianus, Saint Gregory of Nyssa, Saint John Chrysostom, Saint Ephrem of Syria, Saint Hilary of Poitiers, Saint Augustine, Pope Saint Leo the Great, and Saint John of Damascus, to name just a few. As Pope Francis says today, "We become fully human when we become more than human."[11]

We possess as a gift what Christ has by nature. We are not eternal. We are not all-powerful or all-knowing. We are neither uncreated nor infinite. We are not God as Jesus is God, as the Father is God, or as the Spirit is God. Nevertheless, we can truly call God "Abba!" and "Father!" just as the Son has done from all eternity. This is our astounding privilege as God's adopted children.

Deification is the Christian Church's purest expression of salvation by grace. Yet it does not happen without our free assent and cooperation. When Jesus presented the terms of salvation, in chapters 6 and 10 of Saint John's Gospel, many people rejected those terms, and Jesus honored their freedom. God wills all to be saved (1 Timothy 2:4), but he does not compel anyone to be saved.

The *Didache,* like the works of all the Fathers, summons human beings to correspond to God's grace, to choose well, to pass the test, and to live the Way of Life. The greatest of the Western Fathers, Saint Augustine, honored human freedom even as he proclaimed God's sovereign will. Augustine said: "God, who created you without you, will not save you without you."[12]

I was not aware that I was searching for anything so sublime when I began to read the Fathers. I did not know I could reach so high. I did not know the salvation that was available to me inside the Church.

Salvation is divine life we could never reach for ourselves, if God himself had not first reached down to us in Jesus and through his sacraments.

Chapter 5

COMMUNITY

As I read the early Fathers, I worked with my spiritual father to come to a deeper understanding of myself in light of Jesus Christ. In my youthful zeal, I wanted to jump immediately and headfirst into the deep end of the Church. I was ready, I thought, to enter monastic life with an established order or community. Father Martin took it more slowly and suggested that I begin by healing my broken young life. He guided me to work on repairing my relationships with Nancy and our daughter, Amy. I was living hundreds of miles away from them, but it seemed like millions of miles.

Our marriage had, indeed, been a childhood marriage. It might have survived in long-ago times when society supported such unions—or even supported marriage in general. But we were living in a culture that was quickly breaking down. The odds were increasingly against marriage and overwhelmingly against marriage between two teenagers.

The process was painful for all of us. We were a household divided against our wills. We wanted what we believed to be right before God. Yet the more we tried, the greater our failure seemed to be. The more we tried to draw together for the sake of our daughter, the further Nancy and I pushed each other away. Eventually, Nancy asked for a divorce.

When Father Martin saw that there would be no reconciliation, he helped me to work on my friendship with Nancy and my fatherhood to Amy. Nothing would be easy, but he taught me that I could strive to make it simple.

God did not design the human family to be broken, but we break it by our sin. When a household breaks down, as ours did, it has fallen victim to sin. Sometimes the sin is in the divorce. Sometimes the sin is in the attempted marriage—when the couple has willfully tried to create a union that God has not called them to. Nancy and I had done this in many ways. We had married without the real support of our parents, before I was even old enough to give legal consent, and we had fast-forwarded our physical relationship as well.

Eventually, the Church judged that our union was not a valid marriage, and we were granted an annulment. But in that painful year (1977–1978) I did not know that that would be the case, and I could not have anticipated the Church's judgment. I intended to find a way to live as a penitent and repair the spiritual damage I had brought about by my sin—real damage to the lives of others. I wanted to be like the good kings of the Old Testament. I intended to do penance so that the effects of my sins would not be visited upon future generations.

Divorce brings about an almost unbearable isolation. By temperament, I've always been inclined to solitude, but the loneliness of a broken family is not an "elected silence" (to borrow a phrase from the poet Gerard Manley Hopkins). The silence of separation and divorce is not chosen. It's imposed, like a prison sentence. It feels not like a completion, but rather like a rending, a diminishment.

The most famous book by Francis Schaeffer posed the question: *How Should We Then Live?* For me it became a most personal inquiry: How should *I* then live?

Father Martin invited me to live in the house at Alverna, and I took him up on his offer.

I told Father Martin I was ready to become a Franciscan. He smiled. Like Saint Peter at the transfiguration, I didn't know what I was talking about. I wasn't Catholic. I wasn't even baptized. Yet I was sure that I knew what God wanted.

I had tried to force God's hand once before, in my teenage relationship with Nancy. This time, Father Martin kept me from acting impulsively. He advised me to take the spiritual life one step at a time, and to be deliberate and intentional as I gave my life to Jesus. Jesus, he said, would make clear the form my life should take.

The next steps were significant. In 1978 I followed the ancient path of initiation into the Church of Jesus Christ—the Way of Life mapped out in the *Didache*—the rites of grace described in the Acts of the Apostles. On Ash Wednesday of that year I was baptized and confirmed, and I received my first Holy Communion. (Father Martin later told me that he chose that day as a symbol of the cross I would bear in realizing the vision God had given me regarding living in community. He proved to be right, but, like every cross, mine has also brought unimaginable graces.)

I could never, in many lifetimes, earn or deserve a consolation so beautiful. God is merciful. When our earthly homes prove perishable or illusory, he opens the door of his lasting home. He let me take up residence not merely in Alverna, but in his Church, the communion of heaven begun here on earth

———

It was John Chrysostom's lot to live in interesting times. I almost wrote that it was his "misfortune." It is a curse, we are told, to live in interesting times. But we always live in the times that are best for us. Though we might find other eras fascinating—the age of the Fathers or the founding generation of the Franciscans—God has created us to glorify him in the particular circumstances of our lifetime.

To some extent we inherit those circumstances. To some extent we make them.

John Chrysostom was born in the middle of the fourth century. By the time of his birth, Christianity had been legal—and indeed powerful—for decades. In fact, the Church was already experiencing terrible divisions, and nowhere so evident as in his home city of Antioch, where the Arians were vying with the orthodox for dominance. At various times there were three men claiming to be bishop of Antioch, each representing some point on the doctrinal spectrum, from Nicene orthodoxy to Arian heresy. Each of those bishops had his followers, and they were passionate—to the point of brawling in the streets—about the creeds of their faction. The passion took more constructive forms as well. Each faction had its own ascetics, men and women who were consecrated in a particular way to Jesus Christ. In fourth-century Antioch, consecrated virgins and widows numbered in the thousands.

Consecrated life had not yet taken the definite forms we

know today—religious orders with convents and monasteries and codified rules. It was a time of great experimentation. Many people wanted to give their lives to Jesus, and they were looking for authentic ways to do so—ways that were new, perhaps, but faithful to the tradition and in clear continuity with it.

John Chrysostom grew up in the midst of one of these experiments. It was partly the result of choice and partly the result of circumstance.

His mother, Anthousa, was not yet twenty years old when she was left a widow. Her husband, a high-ranking Roman military officer named Secundus, died while she was pregnant with their firstborn. At his death, Anthousa made the decision to consecrate her life to Christ as a widow, after the advice of Saint Paul: "To the unmarried and the widows I say that it is well for them to remain single as I do" (1 Corinthians 7:8). She gave birth to a son, named him John, and raised him in a very pious environment. At some point (and perhaps from the start) they were joined by John's aunt, Sabiniana, a deaconess in the Church (the orthodox faction), whose prayer life was marked by intimacy with God.

Life in this household was almost monastic. Still, Anthousa made sure her son got the best secular education available, enrolling him to study under the great rhetorician Libanius (a pagan), who was the most renowned professor in the world, a teacher of future emperors. Maybe she hoped that John would follow his father into civil service and feather the family's monastic nest for the foreseeable future.

God had other plans.

John excelled at his studies and made friends with similarly brilliant classmates, such as Theodore of Mopsuestia. John and his friends began to dream of living an intensely ascetic life, joining the men who lived as hermits on Mount Silpius at the edge of the city. They discerned this to be a divine calling.

Well, in spite of her piety—and in spite of her own commitment—Anthousa could not bear the thought of John leaving. She already had his future figured out, and she was attached to that narrative. For a while, John compromised with his mother, agreeing to live in community with his friends, devoting their days to study and prayer, but within the safe confines of the city.

They did this for a time, but eventually John's mother gave consent for him to join the ascetics in the wilderness.

There, John lived the life of his choosing. He went long stretches without food, drink, or sleep. He stayed awake through the night, standing with his arms outstretched and committing the books of the Bible to memory. This took a toll on his body. His health began to fail, and eventually the men on the mountain insisted that John return to the city.

Back in Antioch, John presented himself to the bishop for service to the Church. Before long, John was ordained a deacon, and he began preaching, the task that won him renown—and won him his nickname *Chrysostomos,* which means "Golden Mouth."

What was God doing? Apparently, not what John wanted and not what Anthousa wanted. But what then? In childhood John had been formed for monasticism. In adolescence he was driven to solitude. From solitude he had been sent to the city. This series of events must have seemed haphazard at the time, and I'm sure it was frustrating for young John. In retrospect, however—after John's life had run its course—the meaning of each stage would be clear. In all of his detours and seemingly false starts, John was acquiring knowledge, skills, and experience he would not have had otherwise, and they would come in handy as his life reached its crescendo.

John served the orthodox, Catholic community in his home city for a dozen years, first as a deacon and then as a priest. He guided his congregation through many crises, including one instance of seemingly imminent slaughter. He was a father, a good one, too good not to be noticed.

And indeed the emperor, in faraway Constantinople, noticed. He heard that Antioch possessed the Church's greatest preacher, in the person of a simple priest. So he summoned John to serve as bishop of the eastern capital city. John politely declined. He had become attached to his little flock and had no ambitions to be elsewhere.

So the emperor ordered the military to abduct John and take him against his will to Constantinople. They did as they were told. On arriving there, John was ordained bishop, and he accepted it as God's will.

The emperor, however, would come to regret his decision. John preached a radical Gospel, and he decried some of the excesses he saw. He said it was wrong for rich people to have toilet bowls made of precious metals while beggars starved in the streets. He said people were wrongheaded when they donated gold and silver vessels for the liturgy but neglected the poor. But the act that probably voided all his insurance policies was his preaching against the vain use of makeup and fancy dress by certain members of the upper class. John didn't name names, but everyone knew he was talking about the empress.

Like the princess Jezebel in the Old Testament (see 1 Kings

21 and 2 Kings 9), the empress incited her husband first to have John deposed and shamed, then exiled to a harsh land, then exiled to a still harsher land. While on a forced march (by foot) from one indignity to the next, John died. His last words were "Glory be to God for all things!"

John had sought one form of community and then another and then another, but was always driven away or dragged away against his will. He would reach thousands in his congregations—and millions down the years through his books. Yet he died abandoned and alone.

From a purely secular point of view, John's life was a strange tragedy, fodder for the pre-Christian Greeks like Euripides.

To Christians, John's life became a model of vocational fidelity. He is universally honored as a Doctor of the Church.

His life indeed gave glory to God—in all things—in all the twists and turns that John did not want or choose, in all the movements of Providence that he and his mother had resisted. God always had a plan, and each stage proved to be necessary for the next, and certainly necessary for the end. If John had never gone to Mount Silpius, he would probably not have become such a prodigy of fortitude and endurance. He may not have had the stamina to withstand the emperor and the hardships of life in exile. If he had not studied under the great pagan Libanius, he would not have gained the skills that served him well as a pastor, to console his people and to exhort them to a better life.

———

John's attempts at community, like Anthousa's, were experimental. But it was a time of experimentation. Antioch was a crossroads, influencing Rome to the west, Persia to the east, and Egypt to the south. By the middle of the fourth century, the Church in each of these lands had already developed distinctive forms of religious community life. The Persians' tended to be parish-based, immersed in the life of city churches. The Egyptian desert was accommodating solitaries and communities—and sometimes communities of solitaries. All of these communities found ways also to serve others through charitable works. John's lifetime saw the rise of the Church's great health-care institutions, as well as efforts in education and housing.

It was then that Saint Basil the Great founded his monastic community in Cappadocia, and then made it the foundation for renewal in the Church, as he became bishop. Around that time also, John Cassian traveled the world, as Basil had done before him, to survey the various types of monastic communities scattered through Christendom. Their research led to still greater ferment, as monks in Italy and France gained wisdom about communities in the Egyptian desert and in Syrian cities. Great thinkers were able to fuse the experiences of far distant communities, adapt them to new cultural settings, update the details here and there, and present a new synthesis for their time and place.

One such genius was Benedict of Nursia, a sixth-century Father I discovered in my time at Alverna. Benedict was an Italian noble, from old Roman stock. Early in life he was drawn to separate himself from the world, and for years he did so to an increasing extent. It seemed, however, that he always attracted a community of disciples to himself. His life was so serene, he lived such close communion with Christ, that he made others want to have what he had. Over time, the number of religious became so great that Benedict had to establish a rule of common life, a discipline for their life together.

Among the many men who stayed with him, there were some whose intentions sometimes strayed from godly ends. Benedict's companions once tried to poison him rather than follow his counsel. They failed, of course, and he succeeded in founding a religious order that would be a model for future religious communities in the West. Most of those who came later built their rules on his Rule.

The Rule captivated me because of its focus on moderating the extreme practices of some earlier monks. Benedict retained the traditional practices, but adapted them to the times in which he was living—and history shows us that his methods worked very well. I loved the Rule also for its practical approach to keeping silence and maintaining humility in community.

Benedict gave a kind of primacy to liturgical prayer, which he called "God's work." It was the most important labor the monks took up for God; but it was really God who was laboring in them. By fidelity in singing praises to God, the monks kept pure, singing the Word of God together, borne from fast to feast and back again, following the calendar of the Church.

As much as I loved the spontaneity of Francis of Assisi, I was enraptured by the dignity and discipline of Benedict. It seemed to me that these tendencies should not be mutually exclusive, but could rather be complementary. The liturgical piety of a Benedict could and should produce charity and exuberance like that of Francis. (Perhaps this is what earlier reformers, like Basil, were striving for.)

The friars at Alverna put me through a kind of novitiate, to guide me, to educate me, and to test my mettle, too. With my own hands I built a small, sturdy hermitage in the woods, and there I spent my days and nights in prayer and study. Though the place was tiny, my little woodstove barely kept it warm through the Indiana winter. But I didn't care. The cold kept me awake and alert to God's will. I moved through volumes and volumes as the days passed, but I tried to move slowly. I was eager to discern God's movements in my soul, but I was learning not to be overeager.

At regular hours I would join with the friars for their communal praying of the Divine Office—the prescribed sequence of psalms and biblical canticles prayed and sung daily by priests, the religious, and an increasing number of lay Catholics. The Office (also known as the Liturgy of the Hours, or Breviary) includes brief readings from the Old and New Testament as well. I attended Mass and received Communion daily.

I became a Third Order or "Secular" Franciscan, a layman committed to the spirit of Saint Francis. Francis was called the *Poverello*, the "little poor man," because he voluntarily left everything behind to follow Jesus, emptying his purse and stripping himself naked. I wanted to be like him, utterly transparent, possessing nothing but God, who is everything.

Yet I also craved solitude, and I discerned that this, too, would be part of my way through life.

The attraction both to Francis and to a more primitive solitude seemed to be from God. I tested them in spiritual direction with Father Martin. I struggled with them in prayer with God. And I worked them out on paper in the journals I was keeping.

Other details became clear to me. In prayer I began to see

my future in an agrarian community, living evangelical poverty. The community would include married and single members, some of them celibate. The community would be welcoming of non-Catholics, yet would itself be deeply Catholic.

This increasing clarity was exciting me, but it was frightening, too. Though it owed so much to Saint Francis, it was clearly something other than purely Franciscan. There were strains of Saint Benedict's influence. There were gleanings from the Desert Fathers. And there were elements that appeared to be completely new.

Both Father Martin and I saw that I would likely have to "die to Franciscanism" in order to rise to God's call.

But what exactly would that call be? It seemed unlikely that any of the Church's established models could accomplish what I was gradually coming to see. "And no one puts new wine into old wineskins; if he does, the wine will burst the skins, and the wine is lost, and so are the skins; but new wine is for fresh skins" (Mark 2:22).

Under Father Martin's watchful eye, and in dialogue with many new scholar-friends, I put myself through the equivalent of doctoral research in monastic studies.

The phenomenon of "monasticism" predates the Gospel. In the Old Testament we find that certain individuals felt the need—and were called by God—to separate themselves from society in order to draw closer to God. Moses did it. Elijah did it. Jeremiah did it.

Then John the Baptist did it, and so did Jesus. Now, Jesus did not need to remove himself anywhere to get closer to the Father. He did this so that he could set an example of asceticism for Christians. He went to the desert for forty days to fast, pray, and fight against temptation. Every Christian needs to do this to some degree, to find a metaphorical desert for "alone time with God." Every Christian needs to fast and pray. In the Sermon on the Mount, Jesus assumes that all of us will follow him in the ascetic way. He says: "When you fast . . ." (Matthew 6:16, 17) and "When you pray . . ." (Matthew 6:5, 6). He says not "*if*" you fast and pray, but "*when.*"

And his disciples in every generation have fasted and prayed. Some he has called to greater and longer separation than others. Saint Paul spent an extended period in Arabia to prepare for his apostolate. John the Seer was exiled to Patmos, where he took to a cave and beheld the visions of the Apocalypse.

In the time of Christ there were already monastic groups dedicated to prayer and Scripture study. The group that produced the Dead Sea Scrolls was likely a Jewish monastic community. In Alexandria, Egypt, another Jewish group, the Therapeutai, observed celibacy in order to dedicate themselves entirely to God.

Christians took to the ascetical life because Jesus had, and John had, and biblical religion had always made room for those who were called to the solitary way. The word *monk* comes from the Greek word *monos,* "alone."

Monastic movements seemed, to me, to develop along a certain divinely ironic pattern. God would call someone to live apart—someone like Anthony of Egypt or Benedict of Nursia— and no sooner would they be alone than they would begin to attract disciples. Anthony became such a celebrity—and such a draw—that his biographers say that the desert around him soon became a city. It was a city of Christians, each one living alone!

They had been drawn to the life of anchorites, the life of hermits, solitary ascetics, but they found themselves living among other hermits. An intentional society of devout Christians suffers the same problems any earthly society must face; these are consequences of original sin. But Christian ascetics suffer some distinctive problems, too, when they find themselves living in community. How should they interact with one another? And how might they avoid the pitfalls of (on the one hand) overfamiliarity with neighbors and (on the other hand) culpable neglect of those same neighbors? How were they to avoid showing off in their asceticism? Whom should they regard as authorities in their desert dwelling?

It took a former soldier to arrive and impose a kind of order on the life of these desert settlements. Saint Pachomius, in the early fourth century, is often credited with developing the *cenobitical* life, the way of the ascetic living in community. The word *cenobite* comes from the Greek words for "community life." Pachomian monasticism sought to balance the need for solitude with the requirements of living in community.

—

God was overwhelming me with something new. Perhaps I should have been more afraid than I was. But I had seen, along the ancient path, that God is not afraid of new ventures. Benedict, Pachomius, and Anthony (and, much later, Francis) had arrived with new wine, and the Church had helped them to fashion new wineskins that could hold it faithfully. God gave

Anthousa, too, and Chrysostom all that they needed to find their particular way in life. God would provide for me.

Indeed he did. My album *The Lord's Supper* was an unexpected, and spectacular, success. My agent let me know that my share of the royalties that year would likely reach six figures (in 1979 dollars). Meanwhile, my living expenses—as a man who had been striving to live evangelical poverty—were practically zilch.

It was clear to me what I would do with the money. I would do what God had been leading me to do. I would go to live in a larger wood. Years before, when I was touring with the band, I had been drawn to the countryside near Eureka Springs, Arkansas. I would go there, to my desert. And the community would come, too, in God's time.

I would find the community God intended, partly through choice, partly through circumstance, and entirely through grace. I felt certain that there were no fewer seekers in AD 1979 than there had been in 379 or in 79.

Chapter 6

PRAYER OF THE HEART

I N MY TIME AT ALVERNA I ARRIVED AT A DEEPER knowledge of myself, with Father Martin's help. I opened my soul to him through our long walks, our discussions of shared reading, and my sacramental confessions.

I came to know him, too, and his rich personal history. One day he told me about suffering from tuberculosis when he was twenty-four years old. The disease was quite common back then, and very contagious, and when it hit a friary it could take out a lot of friars. It didn't kill Father Martin, but it could have. The doctors removed one of his lungs in order to save his life.

He had always loved to sing. But after he lost that lung he couldn't sustain the notes as before. When I knew him, he sang with gusto—you could see it in his expression—but he would run out of breath on anything longer than a quarter note. Then he'd lapse into a strange sound—like *oh-ho-ho-ho*—because he couldn't get a full breath of air.

There's an old saying in the Church: to sing is to pray twice. It's often attributed to Saint Augustine—though, if he said it, we no longer have his text. Father Martin wanted to pray *a thousand times* through his singing, and he probably succeeded in doing so, even though he couldn't hold the notes. I believe his hymns and psalms were virtuoso performances for the angels, just as they were endearing to me. They were true prayers of the heart. I had sold hundreds of thousands of vinyl recordings of my voice, yet I was merely Father Martin Wolter's apprentice in prayer.

My spiritual father could not pray as he wanted, and that is the mark of a devout soul. Yet he strove to pray as best he could. Saint Paul wrote to the Romans: "we do not know how to pray as we ought, but the Spirit himself intercedes for us with sighs too deep for words" (Romans 8:26). Father Martin sang, confident that the Spirit would take it from there, "For the Spirit helps us in our weakness" (Romans 8:26).

When I remember Father Martin this way, he's an image of my Church: beautiful, filled with grace, desiring all good things—yet hobbled by diseases from its long-ago past. Pope Saint John Paul II often said that the Church must learn again "to breathe with two lungs." He meant that the Church needed to re-integrate the spiritual traditions of the Christian East and the Christian West, estranged now for almost a millennium. Christians have allowed political divisions and cultural differences to keep us from appreciating our common inheritance, the teachings of the Fathers. Instead the East has gone one way and the West another.

In 1987 John Paul wrote: "Such a wealth of praise, built up by the different forms of the Church's great tradition, could help us to hasten the day when the Church can begin once more to breathe fully with her 'two lungs,' the East and the West."[1]

In a later encyclical he said, specifically, that we should find our way to unity along the ancient path, the way of the Fathers, "in the first millennium of the history of Christianity."[2]

The way of the Fathers is a way of prayer, and Father Martin was leading me along that way. In my reading I found treasures buried in books that bore the strangest names on their covers: Evagrius Ponticus, Diadochus of Photiki, Barsanuphius, Dorotheus of Gaza, and John of the Ladder.

They were the early Church Fathers who trained the Christian East in prayer and continue to do so today. Those days when I was living in my hermitage, they were training me. When I first encountered them, their language seemed exotic, but as I tried to practice what they preached I found their way to be as natural as breathing. In fact, they sought to use breathing itself—an inevitable part of human life—as a means and a constant medium of prayer.

Now the thought occurs to me: what better way for us Christians to begin again to *breathe*, as a Church, with both lungs? And maybe we can hold that prayer for more than a quarter note.

———

By the time Diadochus was born (about AD 400), theological arguments about Jesus had been raging for the better part of a century. And they weren't confined to universities. They erupted in shouting matches in the marketplace. Gregory of Nyssa complained that you couldn't ask for change or buy a loaf of bread without someone baiting you for a fight about Jesus. Who was he? Was he really God, as the Father was God? Was he truly human? Was he coeternal, or was he the first and greatest of all creatures? What did he know about himself? And how did he know it?

By the beginning of the fifth century, almost the entire population of the empire was worshipping Jesus. Still, the Church insisted that it wasn't enough just to "sign on the dotted line" as a member of the local church. Doctrine mattered. To give the wrong answers to any of those questions was to worship the wrong Jesus. The Arians worshipped a Jesus who was not truly God. Another group worshipped a Jesus who was not truly human. Yet another worshipped a Jesus who was neither divine nor human, but rather some third thing.

The Church addressed these issues in a series of councils: Nicaea in 325, Constantinople in 381, Ephesus in 431, and Chalcedon in 451. Diadochus, as bishop of Photiki, attended the Council of Chalcedon; the true doctrine of Jesus Christ was his special concern.

We don't know a lot about his life. From his writings we gather that he was, at some point, the leader of a diverse group of ascetics that included cenobites and solitaries. He gave them counsel on advancing in the ways of prayer.

He did not, however, reserve this teaching only for "the elect." Rather, when he was called to be bishop, he set his teaching down for the whole Church.

Diadochus saw the errant doctrine of his time as a subtle poison in the family's water supply. Its speculations were too abstract for ordinary, unlettered folk to sort out. What then was a bishop to do?

The antidote, for Diadochus, was not merely to make people memorize propositions—but to teach them how to draw close to the real Jesus. And whether they were ascetics in the woods or farmhands in the fields, the methods of doing that remained the same.

Diadochus drew from the teachings of the fourth-century Desert Fathers, who promoted the use of simple prayers of aspiration—hardly more than a breath. In Egypt, the most common theme of these short prayers was penitence, sorrow for sins: "Lord, have mercy!"

Diadochus shifted the focus and simplified the prayer. He guided his flock simply to pray the name of Jesus—"nothing but the prayer 'Lord Jesus.'"[3] (This was a method recommended, just a few years earlier, by a letter-writing abbot in Ankara, Saint Neilos.) The holy name, all by itself, Diadochus insisted, would lead Christians from restlessness to stillness. For some, this would provide relief from the speculative itch, which could lead them into heresy. For everyone it could be a path to healing, clarity, charity, and peace.

Again, this method was not an innovation. The Desert Fathers had encouraged the use of aspirations, and Augustine had counseled a busy widow in his parish to imitate the Egyptian hermits in this way. Nor was devotion to the name of Jesus anything new. Saint Paul had long before told the Philippians: "at the *name* of Jesus every knee should bow, in heaven and on earth and under the earth" (2:10). And the pages of the Acts of the Apostles are replete with the primitive Church's devotion to the holy name (see, for example, 2:38, 3:6, 4:10, 8:12, 9:27, etc.). From the first generation, the Church had prescribed Jesus's name for the expulsion of demons, the healing of ailments, and the correction of error.

The goal was to make Jesus the single focal point of life, and to make our prayer to him as constant as breath. Breathe in: *Lord*. Breathe out: *Jesus*.

It's not mechanical. It's not magical. It's love. People do heroic things for love. They give up drinking or drugs or gambling, but the way they overcome is by keeping their beloved in mind when faced with temptation. So they're faced with a stark choice between the loved one or the vice. If our prayer is *Jesus,* we will have him always before us. We will have the habit of preferring nothing to him. And, like the apostles, we can do all things in him who strengthens us (Philippians 4:13) and in his holy name.

In the two centuries after the death of Saint Diadochus, the prayer underwent further development, becoming a compact creed: "Lord Jesus Christ, Son of God, have mercy on me, a sinner." That simple formula includes elements of adoration, contrition, and supplication. It confesses Jesus's divinity and our own sinfulness. It's as hard as diamond, but it rises lightly as breath. It has sustained the inner life of ascetics and ordinary folk in the Eastern churches for well over a millennium.

———

What was Jesus asking of me as I entered a new phase of my life? I couldn't make out the far horizon, but the next step seemed clear enough from my reading in the New Testament. It just seemed impossible, that's all.

He seemed to think that I "ought always to pray" (Luke 18:1). Saint Paul chimed in with the same idea: "pray without ceasing" (Ephesians 6:18; see also 1 Thessalonians 5:17).

It would take little effort for me to explain these passages away and minimize their impact. But I'm fairly sure that, at least in my case, that would be an evasion. The Holy Spirit impresses certain words upon us, and we're bound to confront them.

The Eastern Fathers offered a way to approach the problem. How can we pray when there's so much else we have to get done? We can key our prayer to our every breath.

Though my life in solitude had so far been very Franciscan—

and, thus, very Western—this "Eastern approach" seemed a beautiful complement, a completion. Pope Saint John Paul would eventually give me the metaphor: I was breathing with both lungs.

That year of my solitude, 1979, the ancient texts on the Jesus Prayer were collected for the first time in English translation. The anthology, called the *Philokalia* (Greek for "love of the beautiful"), had been compiled by Orthodox monks in the eighteenth century. Excerpts had appeared earlier and had deeply affected authors as diverse as Thomas Merton and J. D. Salinger. Now the first volume, which included the most ancient texts on this type of prayer, appeared in splendid English—and it deeply affected me.

The Eastern Fathers tell us to invoke the name and person of Jesus with every breath we take. Think about it: breathing is the only analogue we have as we begin to consider the scriptural command. It's the one thing we do without ceasing. If we're living, we're breathing. When we stop breathing, we're dead.

It's a fitting analogue because, as we know from Saint Paul, our prayer is a work of the Spirit. Prayer is not something we could do on our own. God is transcendent. He is wholly "other" from us. But he gives us his Spirit to pray within us, so we can say with Jesus, "Abba! Father!" In both Hebrew and Greek, the word for "breath" and "Spirit" is one and the same—in Hebrew, *ruah;* in Greek, *pneuma.* Prayer is possible because we have the breath of God.

Pray without ceasing, the Fathers tell us with Saint Paul. Unite every breath to God. I learned in my time in the hermitage that I could not keep parts of life purely for myself, apart from God. If I did that, I was preparing a room for sin. If I could pray from the heart, if I could pray with every breath, I would leave myself no opportunity to build a reservation for self and sin. I would sooner stop breathing. I would sooner die.

Eastern Christians sometimes pray the Jesus Prayer the way Western Christians pray the Rosary. They recite the words, "Lord Jesus Christ, Son of God, have mercy on me, a sinner," while they count the recitations on a string of beads or knots.

Some people worry that this is the sort of repetition that Jesus warned against, in the Sermon on the Mount, when he said: "And in praying do not heap up empty phrases as the Gentiles do; for they think that they will be heard for their many words" (Matthew 6:7). The Lord here confirmed the oracles of the prophet Isaiah, who had inveighed against those who honor the Lord with the tongue, while their hearts are far from him (see Isaiah 29:13). Jesus will have none of that, and so he speaks of such empty prayer with words that denote stuttering or babbling mindlessly.

But nothing could be further from Jesus's prohibition than the Jesus Prayer. It has few phrases, each of them just a few words, and none of them is "empty." As Eastern Christians move along their beads, they heap up phrases that are full of meaning and laden with love.

Jesus gave his warning against vain repetition as a prelude to his unveiling of the perfect prayer: the Lord's Prayer, the "Our Father." Christians in every generation have considered the Lord's Prayer not simply a model for prayer, but as a prayer to be repeated many times over the course of a faithful lifetime. It is significant that the *Didache* exhorted first-century Christians to pray the "Our Father" three times every day.

Not all repetition is vain. As a musician—and as a man

whose aging body requires exercise—I know that reps can be beneficial, can make me more limber, can make me better at a given task. When that task is prayer, we should all want to make progress. We should all hope to improve. It can help us to go over the same ground, not in a rush, not mindlessly, but rather meditatively.

It can be good, in fact, to take it very slowly now and then, repeating the Jesus Prayer one word at a time, savoring each word slowly, considering it in God's presence and asking for his light.

—

The Fathers teach us to unite the Jesus Prayer with our breathing, and breathing takes place in two motions. We inhale, and we exhale. So the masters divide the Jesus Prayer into two motions. With the intake, we say, "Lord Jesus Christ, Son of God"; and then with the outflow, we say, "Have mercy on me, a sinner."

As we inhale, we fill our lungs up, and so symbolically we fill our spirit—with Jesus, the Lord and Christ!

Then, as we exhale, we're letting go. We're separating ourselves from sin by our confession that we are sinners and our plea for mercy.

To meditate on the words is not to obsess intellectually. But it's important to know what the words mean so that we're intuiting the meaning as we pray.

The first word is *Lord*. It is a confession of Jesus's Godhead, his deity, his true divinity. *Lord* is the word the English translations use to render the Hebrew tetragrammaton, YHWH, the unpronounceable four-letter abbreviation for God's name. When we say "Jesus is Lord," we are accepting the claims that got him crucified (see John 5:18). Jesus called himself "I AM," the divine name that God had revealed to Moses (see Exodus 3:14; John 8:58). Saint Paul knew how provocative it would be to call Jesus Lord, yet he presented "Jesus is Lord" as a saving act of faith (see Romans 10:9)—and even itself a divine action, a work of the Holy Spirit (see 1 Corinthians 12:3).

Pronouncing the name of God was forbidden to Jews, and even Gentile Christians in the early Church respected that taboo. They replaced it with titles of respect that they customarily applied to human nobility and royalty—*Kyrios* and *Dominus*, the Greek and Latin equivalents of the English *Lord*.

When we follow the early Christians in praying to Jesus as "Lord," we are implicitly rejecting the doctrine of the heretic Arius, who denied Jesus's coeternity and drew a distinction between Jesus and the God who revealed himself as "I am."

We are also implicitly rejecting the doctrine of the second-century heretic Marcion, who also made a distinction between the God of the New Testament and the YHWH of the Old Testament. While Arius held that Jesus was *inferior* to YHWH, Marcion taught that Jesus was infinitely *superior* to YHWH. Marcion saw the entire Old Testament as a fraud perpetrated by a demonic demiurge who was diametrically opposed to the God of Jesus.

The Church Fathers rejected both views and affirmed the apostolic faith in three divine persons, coequal and coeternal—affirming as well the unity of the Old Testament and the New. We join our voice with theirs simply by addressing Jesus as "Lord."

We address him, too, by his name: Jesus. *Yeshua. Jehoshua. Joshua. Iesous.* You'll find the name rendered differently in various languages and dialects. Its Hebrew root means simply "YHWH saves." In Saint Matthew's Gospel, we learn that Jesus's name was revealed to Saint Joseph by an angel: "you shall call his name Jesus, for he will save his people from their sins" (Matthew 1:21). Even to name Jesus is to acknowledge him as Savior and implicitly ask for salvation. Salvation is something we cannot achieve on our own. We are sinners (as we acknowledge on the exhale). We've fallen, and we can't get up.

The Christian religion is not a theological philosophy. It's not an academic discipline we can master in order to pass the test. That's how another ancient Christian heresy, Gnosticism, treated religion. The Gnostics said that Jesus came to disclose the secret to escaping the suffering that's part and parcel of life in the created cosmos. Once we knew the secret, we could use it as a password to get by the "Archons," who were the sadistic gatekeepers of the world. All we had to do was to amass the knowledge and pass the test. The Gnostics were utterly rejected by those who knew the apostolic teaching. Saint Irenaeus of Lyons—who received the faith from Saint Polycarp, who received it from the apostle John—dedicated his ministry to rooting out this corrosive heresy. *Heresy* comes from the Greek word for "choice," and the choice of bad doctrine is always a choice that brings division, in the self as well as in the Church.

Knowledge puffs up, Saint Paul said (see 1 Corinthians 8:1). If salvation were a matter of memorizing formulas, we'd just program it into a calculator and be mighty proud of ourselves. But that's not how it works. The truth is that we need a Savior, and God became man for the sake of our salvation. He chose for himself a name that would reveal his role. Simply to speak his name is to pray deeply.

Christ, from the Greek *Christos,* renders the Hebrew word *Moshiach,* which means "Anointed One." It's not Jesus's surname—not his family name. It's his title. He's the Messiah. God the Father has chosen him and sent him forth on a mission. That's how much God loved the world: he sent his only Son to save it.

Jesus is *the* Christ, but others had been anointed before him—designated by God for a special status or role. As an outward sign of their election, God's chosen ones—priests, prophets, and kings—received an anointing with oil. These events in the Old Testament foreshadowed the Messiah of the New Testament, and they were fulfilled in him. Jesus was anointed not with oil, but with the Holy Spirit. He is the definitive Christ.

Again, when we confess him as such, when we call him Christ, we are implicitly rejecting the false saviors of the heretics. The Christ was anointed by YHWH, in fulfillment of the prophecies of the Old Testament.

Jesus, the Christ, is the "Son of God." And here, too, we should pray slowly, so that we regain the radical, original sense of the claim that got Jesus killed. To be God's "Son" is to be God's equal. It is to be the same sort of being as God. As human beings, you and I can have only human beings as our children. We cannot give birth to any other sort of animal. We cannot adopt any other, nonhuman creatures as our children. The zookeeper can keep all sorts of beasts in his menagerie, and he might grow quite fond of them. He might like them more than he likes his fellow humans. But he cannot legally (or sanely) call them his true children.

When we address Jesus as "Son of God," we are professing his divinity. We are implicitly acknowledging the Trinity: the plurality of persons in the Godhead. As Tertullian saw in the second century, we did not know God as the eternal Father till we met the eternal Son in Jesus.[4]

We are saying, moreover, that God is love—a certain deep kind of love that is recognizable in family relationships. The eternal form of this love is God. The love shared among the three persons of the Trinity is an eternal love that is the model for the love in all human families.

Have mercy, we go on to pray, and so we return once again to the theme of our salvation. We need mercy because we are sinners. Only God can save us because only he is holy. God shares his fatherly love by adopting us as children—sons and daughters in the eternal Son. God has saved us by taking flesh and dying on a cross so that we might be born again and become a new creation in Jesus. There is no greater love than laying down one's life for a friend, and that is what our loving God has done most perfectly. In his mercy, he shared our life so that we might share his life.

Jesus. Christ. Son of God. By praying the Jesus Prayer slowly and thoughtfully, we recover the shocking sense of these traditional phrases. For too many Christians, these words have become shopworn, or obscured by centuries of gilding. The Jesus Prayer gives us a chance to encounter them anew—and be transformed by them.

The Jesus Prayer also inoculates us against the many Christological heresies, which unfortunately did not expire at the end of the first millennium. The propositions condemned by the ancient councils have all re-emerged in the last century or so, rephrased by theologians at accredited Christian institutions. The cut-and-paste versions of Jesus—proposed by Marcion, Arius, and their ilk—continue to re-appear and lure people away from the demands of the true Gospel.

Diadochus knew better—and he wanted the best for his flock. In a distracted age, he showed them a way to train their focus on Jesus Christ. He is God, "rich in mercy" (Ephesians 2:4), and he gives mercy to those who ask. Jesus himself rehearsed the exchange, and it appears in the Gospels:

> As he drew near to Jericho, a blind man was sitting by the roadside begging; and hearing a multitude going by, he inquired what this meant. They told him, "Jesus of Nazareth is passing by."
>
> And he cried, "Jesus, Son of David, have mercy on me!"
>
> And those who were in front rebuked him, telling him to be silent; but he cried out all the more, "Son of David, have mercy on me!"
>
> And Jesus stopped, and commanded him to be brought to him; and when he came near, he asked him, "What do you want me to do for you?"
>
> He said, "Lord, let me receive my sight."
>
> And Jesus said to him, "Receive your sight; your faith has made you well."
>
> And immediately he received his sight and followed him, glorifying God; and all the people, when they saw it, gave praise to God. (Luke 18:35-43)

Jesus of Nazareth is still passing by!

The Jesus Prayer, as formulated by Diadochus and the other Fathers, is not a mere intellectual exercise. It is a cry from the heart from helpless beggars who cannot lift themselves up: *Lord! Jesus! Son of David—Son of God! Have mercy on me!*

It did not fail the beggar beside the road, and it will not fail to draw divine mercy down upon us. We should pray it with all our heart. We should sing it in order to pray it twice. We should pray it with gusto, with both lungs.

Chapter 7

THE PUBLIC WORK

LREADY IN ALVERNA I FOUND MYSELF IN A
growing community. I'm no Anthony of Egypt, and
I'm no Benedict of Nursia, but my God is their God,
and his ways remain constant. Though I had withdrawn to be
alone with him, he soon drew others to share our company. We
were becoming a community, and it was clear that we would
soon have to do as Pachomius did and find ways—and an accommodating place—to share life together.

Looking back on that time, I identify with two men of the
fourth century, Basil the Great and John Cassian, because both
traveled from place to place taking careful note of the local monastic establishments and religious forms of life. I was doing
that, too, in my way. I was reading widely in history, culture,
and geography, studying the ways of common life of every tradition on earth, Christian and non-Christian. I also began to visit
monastic communities, ranging from mendicant Franciscan
communities and communal Benedictine and Cistercian communities to the semi-eremitical Camaldolese and Carthusian
communities.

The people who made their way to Alverna also represented
a variety of backgrounds. Many had experienced profound

conversions through the Catholic Charismatic Renewal, which was then burgeoning in the American Midwest, and at Protestant Pentecostal churches. Many, too, had a background similar to my own, in the Jesus Movement and American evangelicalism.

As I ranged in my reading, I recognized the phenomenon, and I looked for organizational principles, sorting through the distinctive traits of ancient Celtic and Egyptian communities as well as the medieval Italian and French forms. I searched also for traits that were common, and none was so ubiquitous and so foundational as the love of good liturgy.

It's always there in the great monastic communities. The first Fathers of the Egyptian desert may have lived as solitaries, but they had to make arrangements for regular visits from a priest. They had to gather for the common assembly. They called it the *synaxis*, Greek for "drawn together," and the liturgy was the magnet that drew the disparate and distant ascetics into Christian community for the Eucharist once a week (or more often, depending on the availability of clergy).

Basil's later monastic community (like Augustine's, still later) was different. It was urban, and he was the bishop, so he counted on his ascetics to take up a liturgical reform that would serve as the engine of social reform. The brothers and sisters would first of all pray well. Then their prayer would transform city life in Caesarea.

The Mass, after all, is the *public work* of the Church. That's the literal meaning of the Greek word at the root of *liturgy*: *leitourgia*. It's a necessary public work, like common access to water or the maintenance of roads. God's people need liturgy in order to be a people, and not just a database of names stored somewhere in heaven. This has been the way of Christian community from the beginning. What Christians do is *gather*—to share the apostolic teaching, the communion, the breaking of the bread, and the prayers.

This was all pretty new to me. My Christian experiences had been largely individualistic—all about me—and they were informal in the extreme, coming as I did from the Jesus Movement. Like most movements from the sixties we tended to emphasize spontaneity, improvisation, free form, and personal style. The very word *ritual* suggested rigidity to us: restrictive forms, hidebound traditions, rote and mindless repetition of words that had long since lost their meaning. We gathered for church, but that gathering was really secondary to our individual relationship with Jesus.

As I read in the Fathers, however, I began to see how ritual public worship had always been the way of God's people. In biblical religion, the public and personal were not separate and opposed, but rather complementary dimensions of a single, unified, integrated life. Much of the Old Testament—the Law, the Prophets, and the Writings—is taken up with questions of how to offer sacrifice the right way. God is intensely and constantly concerned with Israel's ways of worship. He wants beautiful liturgy to express, and then to inspire, a just and faithful life.

For the Fathers as for the apostles, the central act of worship was the celebration of the Eucharist. Just after the first century turned to the second, Ignatius of Antioch wrote: "Take heed, then, to have but one Eucharist. For there is one flesh of our Lord Jesus Christ, and one cup to show forth the unity of his blood; one altar; as there is one bishop, along with the presbytery and deacons, my fellow servants: that so, whatsoever you do, you may do it according to the will of God."[1]

I wanted to understand this life of worship, so I was drawn especially to the works of the Fathers that elucidated the mysteries. I learned that there is a Greek word just to describe those works. They are works of *mystagogia*—mystagogy—a pedagogy, or teaching, about the mysteries. For the clergy of the Church are "stewards of the mysteries of God" (1 Corinthians 4:1).

The Latin equivalent term for the English word *mystery* is *sacramentum*—sacrament. We have come to understand sacraments as outward and visible signs of grace that is invisible and spiritual. That "mystery" is pre-eminently true in Jesus, the Word made flesh, but also in the signs of his life that he established in the Church. The mysteries are Jesus's means of sharing his life with us.

I found mystagogical elements in the New Testament, especially as Jesus discoursed on the Bread of Life and Saint Paul walked the Corinthians through the dos and don'ts of the eucharistic rite. That method is there also in a scattershot way in the works of the Apostolic Fathers, especially Clement, Ignatius, and Pseudo-Barnabas. But it comes to the fore in the fourth century, when the Church was at last enjoying its freedom, and great crowds came to ask for baptism. The bishops instructed the aspiring Christians in biblical doctrine and morals, but the last and most important lessons were reserved for sacramental mystagogy. Among the ancient Fathers best known for their mystagogy are Cyril of Jerusalem, Ambrose of Milan, Augustine of Hippo, Theodore of Mopsuestia, John Chrysostom, Pseudo-Dionysius the Areopagite, and Maximus the Confessor.

I devoured their works. Most were composed as homilies, and they simply walked step-by-step through the sacramental rites, explaining the prayers and gestures along the way. These

ancient sermons spoke to me across the centuries and were enormously helpful to me as a new Catholic—and a Christian new
to liturgical worship. I knew the Bible pretty well, so I could
recognize the "Holy, Holy, Holy" from the Old Testament book
of Isaiah and the New Testament book of Revelation. But men
like Cyril explained what it meant *in the context of earthly worship.* Why were mere mortals now permitted to sing the songs
of angels? What about the sign of peace? What did that do for
the Church, beside spread colds and the flu? The Fathers showed
me that all these earthly movements expressed realities that
were heavenly. Everything I saw and heard reflected something
unseen and beyond hearing. All this was a consequence of the
Church's incarnational faith. The Word was made flesh, and
God had empowered the material of the world—bread, wine,
water, and oil—to convey true spiritual power, true spiritual life.

This had an immediate effect on my work. As I grew in my
experience of the liturgy, I came to compose many musical settings for the prayers and responses of the Mass. I couldn't help it.

—

Liturgy is the public work of the Church. The liturgical *synaxis*
is the assembly, the in-gathering of any Christian community.
It's the property the Church holds in common. It's what we
share.

Liturgy is the place where we gather and worship. As we
worship together, we build each other up in Christ according
to a pattern that is ancient and time-tested. It's not the passing
fancies of individuals or particular cultures. It meets the needs
of everyone in any time. It is universal. It is Catholic.

So Catholics love the Mass. We love to love it—and we love

to criticize it. Now, most of our criticism is positive and meant to be constructive . . . but not all of it. And this should not be surprising. Since the Mass is the *public* work of the Church, it's the thing that's most exposed—and thus most exposed to criticism.

It has always been that way. I'm sure that the villagers who sat beside the Holy Family at synagogue were prone to complain, now and then, about the way the rabbi conducted the service—how it wasn't like the old days—or how it was *too much* like the old days and wasn't current with the latest trends of the religious establishment in Jerusalem or the outliers in Qumran.

When Saint Paul sat down to write his First Epistle to the Corinthians, he was dealing with a lot of problems, but he traced many of them to bad liturgy. He condemns liturgical abuses in the strongest terms. He goes so far as to say they're making people sick to death.

When we look back to the age of the Fathers, and when we read the Fathers' mystagogical homilies, we can sometimes allow ourselves to form romantic impressions about the ancient liturgies. We can dream that every priest was a spiritual giant like John Chrysostom, chanting from memory (and always on key) as he strode through glorious and billowy clouds of incense. We can persuade ourselves that every parish church was decorated with icons as stunning as those that have survived the centuries, from St. Catherine's at Mount Sinai and San Vitale in Ravenna.

The evidence, however, shows a different church—a church that should be more familiar to us. When John Chrysostom preached about First Corinthians, he used the occasion to nag his congregation about their participation in the liturgy: "If you don't come to edify your brother, why do you come here at all?"[2] The great Jesuit historian Robert Taft has cataloged Chrysostom's many gripes about the liturgical failures of his day. It's an extensive catalog. Chrysostom accuses his congregation of restless roaming during the rites; of ignoring the preacher—or showing their exasperation with him; of talking during the readings; of arriving late and leaving early. The young men, he said, looked like frantic stallions as they chased the young women through the congregation. The young women, for their part, painted themselves like harlots and dressed like they were going to nightclubs. At different times, Chrysostom said his congregation's behavior was suited more to the barbershop, or a sporting event, or a tavern, or a bordello.[3] Taft has no trouble producing numerous examples from the great man's preaching.

John Chrysostom was hardly alone in his griping. Many of his brother clergy were right there with him. And we can bet that their congregations gave as eagerly as they got—that the layfolk, too, were ready critics of their parish liturgies. The only difference is that the laity (for better and for worse) did not have equal opportunities to publish their complaints for all the ages.

We honor men like Hippolytus of Rome, Basil of Caesarea, John Chrysostom, and Gregory the Great because they were liturgical *reformers*. They challenged their congregations to engage more deeply and personally in the Church's great act of worship. And the number of such reformers is legion. From this we must conclude that the liturgy is often, if not always, in need of reform. In the nineteenth century, men like Prosper Guéranger revived interest in the Fathers in the hope that patristic liturgy would renew modern liturgy. Popes Pius X and Pius XII took up the same project as they encouraged scholarship of the Fathers and the early liturgies.

The call is always out for liturgical reform, and it's probably always needed. In our own day we hear from Catholic progressives who say they get hives from Gregorian chant and can't bear to have a priest turn his back on them. From the other side, we hear from hyper-traditionalists who say they have a strong suspicion that the Mass in use since 1970 is invalid. We also hear from the vast majority in the middle who just want a richer and more personal encounter with Jesus Christ and with others when they go to Mass.

Ours is a big Church, and it has room for both extremes and every shade of liturgical opinion in between. The struggle between tradition and progress makes for a good dynamic, a creative tension. We hold ourselves accountable to the past. We have been given our heritage as a trust. Yet an important part of that heritage is periodic liturgical reform—sometimes quite extensive. And another important inheritance is the model of enculturation we find in the missionary work of the ancient Fathers. The liturgy celebrated by the Maronites in Lebanon looks, sounds, and smells significantly different from the Mass in a typical American Latin Rite parish, but the priests at both altars are presiding over the same eucharistic feast. The essentials are the same, though the rite has changed as it has moved from place to place and from time to time.

When we feel the urge to bash the liturgy, we should ask how we might change ourselves first. How might we improve our dispositions at Mass? How might we make our own participation fuller, more conscious, and more active?

In the pages that follow, I will "walk through" a typical liturgy as it plays out in a typical parish in my country. If you travel to Beirut, or Kerala, or Kiev, or Athens, or Jerusalem, you may encounter a liturgy that is strikingly different—in language, in the use of music, in the style of church decoration, and in the order of prayers—but all of the Church's eucharistic liturgies are fundamentally the same, composed (since the first century) of the same basic elements. Certainly there has been development and elaboration over the centuries. From ancient times there have been many liturgical families in the Church—Malabar, Melkite, Maronite, Chaldean, Ambrosian, and Mozarabic, to mention just a few. The liturgy always finds a form that will fulfill the varying needs of different peoples. But there is only one Eucharist.

—

Saint Paul wrote to the Thessalonians: "May the God of peace himself sanctify you wholly; and may your spirit and soul and body be kept sound and blameless at the coming of our Lord Jesus Christ. The one who calls you is faithful. And he will also accomplish it" (1 Thessalonians 5:23-24).

Liturgy is public work, the work of the people. But remember, too, that Saint Benedict called the liturgy the "work of God." Insofar as it is our work, it involves our whole being: body, soul, and spirit. Since it is God's work, it involves his whole being, so it could not be more reliable: he is faithful; he will accomplish what he sets out to do, which is to sanctify us—make us holy by sharing his own holiness with us, mixing his flesh and blood with ours.

It's common, I'm sure, for everyone to think of worship as an act of the human soul and spirit. But the body? That's where a lot of people get uncomfortable—especially Western Christians since the Protestant Reformation. We like to think of religion in terms of faith, not works, and faith belongs to the realm of soul and spirit, mind and will. But it's not that simple because we're composite beings, simultaneously spiritual and material, and we're not quite ourselves if one of those components is missing. God wants to sanctify not just part of us, but all of us. Saint Paul probably foresaw this danger as he exhorted the Romans: "I appeal to you therefore, brethren, by the mercies of God, to *present your bodies* as a living sacrifice, holy and acceptable to God, *which is your spiritual worship*" (Romans 12:1). That's amazing. Our worship isn't truly spiritual unless our bodies get in on the act!

In the liturgy—and then in life—we try to practice what Saint Paul called "the obedience of faith" (Romans 1:5, 16:26). It's not just a mental exercise; it's not just a movement of neurons. It involves the whole person, hands and tongues and hearts expressing the effects of grace on the will.

Saint Paul spoke of this in priestly, sacrificial terms. He called himself "a minister (*leitourgos*) of Christ Jesus to the Gentiles in priestly (*hierourgeō*) service of the gospel of God, so that the offering of the Gentiles may be acceptable, sanctified by the Holy Spirit" (Romans 15:16).

And we, too, participate in that same priesthood, through our baptism (1 Peter 2:5, 9; Revelation 1:6). With Christ, we're offering his body. In Christ, we're offering our bodies, too.

The Fathers of the Church understood this in a deep way. They understood it in their bones. Our African friend Tertullian, who lived in the second century, went so far as to say that our bodies were made for this purpose. They were made for true worship of God, in obedience to the commands of Jesus Christ. "You have been given a mouth for eating and for drinking?" he asked. "Why not rather for . . . praising God?"[4]

In the liturgy, in the obedience of faith, we obey Christ: "This is my Body. . . . Do this in remembrance of me. . . . Eat my flesh. . . . Drink my blood. . . . Rise with me, bodily!"

For Catholics the experience is physical from the start. Saint Maximus the Confessor said the very act of opening the door of the Church is symbolic—leaving the world behind and entering heaven.

Then we dive in with a splash. We dip our hands in the holy water font. It's an action that the Fathers knew well. They learned it from the apostles, who learned it as Jews. "I desire then that in every place the men should pray, lifting holy hands," said Saint Paul (1 Timothy 2:8). "Holy hands" are hands that are clean and purified. It was a custom of Jews to observe a symbolic washing before beginning to pray. God's people never left this practice behind. Eusebius describes a fourth-century church with a lavish fountain for this purpose at the front entrance. An Egyptian book of prayers, the so-called Sacramentary of Serapion of Thmuis, was compiled around the same time and includes a traditional blessing for holy water.

We dip our hands in holy water and we trace a cross over our body. Few practices are so well attested in the ancient sources as this one. It is likely that the sign of the cross is the "seal" on the forehead referred to in the book of Revelation (7:3ff). Indeed, all the earliest sources indicate that the first Christians simply traced the sign on their foreheads rather than over their head and trunk the way we do today.

The early Christians loved to make this sign. Tertullian said they had the habit of making it everywhere: "In all our travels and movements, in all our coming in and going out, in putting on our shoes, at the bath, at the table, in lighting our candles, in lying down, in sitting down, whatever task occupies us, we mark our foreheads with the Sign of the Cross."[5] They made the sign of the cross even in public! Imagine how strange that must have seemed. Not only were they professing an illegal religion—an act that by itself could probably get them arrested and martyred—but they were tracing over their bodies the instrument of the most horrific and humiliating public torture that the Romans could imagine.

Saint Cyril of Jerusalem said: "Let us then not be ashamed to confess the Crucified. Be the cross our seal, made with boldness by our fingers on our brow."[6] The sign of the cross is always a sign of contradiction, a countercultural act. We use it to begin our public worship.

Holy water and the cross—these are symbols of our baptism, of our dying and rising with Christ. So this simple act evokes all those images and customs.

I've lingered a long time over this simple, quick action, which most Catholics perform automatically. I've done this to show the richness that's in every gesture and phrase in the eucharistic liturgy, even those that are seemingly simple. If I wanted to (and if I sincerely thought enough readers were interested), I could probably produce a book only on the sign of the cross and the use of holy water, the historical development of these practices and their meaning.

The Church Fathers unpacked our liturgical actions in book-length treatises. This chapter—indeed this book—does not afford us the same opportunity. Our discussion will be necessarily brief, and for this may God forgive me, and may my readers be inspired to seek out the great mystagogical works of the Fathers.

———

As our sign of the cross invokes the Trinity, so do the opening prayers of the Mass, which are usually taken from Saint Paul (see 2 Corinthians 13:13). The *Catechism of the Catholic Church* (n. 234) tells us: "The mystery of the Most Holy Trinity is the central mystery of Christian faith and life. It is the mystery of God in himself. It is therefore the source of all the other mysteries of faith, the light that enlightens them." It is the light that illumines the Mass for us.

If we recognize that we are in the presence of the one true God, then we must also recognize that we are not God. He is good, and we have sinned. He is holy, and we have sinned against him. He made us in his image, and we have desecrated those icons by our thoughts, words, and deeds, our actions and omissions.

It's logical for us, then, to proceed to the penitential rite. We pray the prayer that's so often repeated in Scripture: Lord, have mercy! My bishop, who is a Greek scholar, likes to point out that we use the "vocative case"; we are addressing ourselves to the Lord, not simply talking about him. So it's a short prayer and a cry from the heart. We repeat it three times, with a slight variation, addressing him once as "Christ" rather than "Lord."

We may also confess our sins in a longer prayer called the *Confiteor*, the Latin equivalent of its opening phrase: "*I confess* to almighty God. . . ." It is a prayer that is powerful for its brief but subtle study of the tortuous ways of the human heart (Jeremiah 17:9). We sin by what we do and what we fail to do, sometimes by our words and other times by our cowardly silence, sometimes by being a busybody and other times by our neglect. For all this we ask forgiveness and healing.

We move, then (at least on feast days and Sundays outside Lent), to singing the Gloria: "Glory to God in the highest, and on earth peace to people of good will. . . ." The foundation of this prayer is the hymn the heavenly hosts sang when Jesus was born. It entered the liturgy early on; the Fathers record that the Church in Rome was using it for Christmas Masses in the first century. The Mass is an appropriate setting for the Gloria, because during the Mass once again God the Son is touching down, enfleshed, upon the earth. Once again, the heavenly hosts are gathering with men and women to celebrate that fact.

After the Gloria come the readings from Scripture, and I know very few Christian bodies that require so much of the Bible to be read in every single service. On Sundays our readings usually include a selection from the Old Testament, then a psalm, followed by a portion of the non-Gospel New Testament, concluding with an episode from the Gospel. And the readings are prescribed so that no biblical books are neglected over the course of a three-year cycle.

The readings are heard and acknowledged as "the Word of the Lord" and "the Gospel of the Lord." Thus the congregation recognizes their divine authority, and every worshipper holds himself or herself accountable for fidelity to that Word.

The congregation heralds the Gospel reading with a special biblical acclamation: *Alleluia!* It means "Praise the Lord," and it is a liturgical prayer the ancient Jews associated with Passover. At the paschal sacrifice in the Temple, the tribe of priests, the Levites, chanted the psalms known as the Hallel Psalms

(Psalms 113–118). *Hallel* means "praise," and we know it from *Hallelujah.* We sing it as "Alleluia!" At the Passover banquet, families would chant two of those psalms (113 and 114; see Matthew 26:30 and Mark 14:26).

Alleluia! The inclusion of this Hebrew word in every Mass—in every language—is our way of recognizing, as Saint Paul said to the Corinthians, that "Christ our paschal lamb has been sacrificed" (1 Corinthians 5:7). Therefore, we can go forward to "celebrate the festival . . . with the unleavened bread of sincerity and truth" (1 Corinthians 5:8).

The Mass, then, is the sacrifice of the new Passover, the Passover of Jesus Christ, the Lamb of God (John 1:29, 36). Jesus's sacrifice is "once for all," as we read many times in the New Testament (Hebrews 7:27, etc.), but the offering is eternal. It is the Son's self-offering to the Father, and it is re-presented in every Mass. Jesus is not "crucified again," as some anti-Catholic polemicists charge. In fact, that very idea is repudiated in the old *Baltimore Catechism,* which for much of the last century was the American Church's primary teaching tool.

Nevertheless, the Lamb appears "as if slain" (Revelation 5:6), and we celebrate his everlasting Passover. Like the old Passover, it is a passage from slavery to freedom, from sin to virtue—but now also from death to divine life.

The homily follows, when our clergy open up the meaning of the Scriptures we've just read. Our preachers are commissioned to speak in the name of the Church. Thus they are bound not to dazzle us with their rhetoric, but rather confront us with the truth. In the early Church, not every priest and deacon was licensed to preach. It was a special privilege. It is still a privilege given by the Church in trust. The word that the priest or deacon speaks must be not his own, but Christ's. He must never contradict the teaching of the Church or the faith as it has been received. But if he wants to inspire, he must preach with faith-filled fire.

We profess our faith, after the homily, using an ancient formula, usually the creed of the Councils of Nicaea and Constantinople, though we may also use the older Roman baptismal creed, known as the Apostle's Creed. These creeds were devised by the Fathers themselves to be our protection against heresies about Christ, the Trinity, and the Church.

Forward we go to the petitions and intercessions of the Mass. We present our community's urgent needs before the Lord, and for these intentions we offer the Lord's sacrifice.

What has happened up to this point is known as the "Liturgy of the Word." What follows is the "Liturgy of the Eucharist," the portion of the rite that is properly sacrificial.

And, really, this is why we've come to church. Catholics don't go to Mass for singing, preaching, or entertainment. Sometimes the music's good, and sometimes it's not. Sometimes the preaching is good; sometimes it's not. It's good when it's all good. God deserves our best—and the liturgy is, after all, our "public work" for him! But, primarily, it's his public work for us. It's *opus Dei,* God's work. And that sacrificial work of Christ our High Priest is what God is up to in the Liturgy of the Eucharist.

The ministry of music may be bad, the ministry of preaching may be wanting, but Jesus always shows up.

Read the Epistle to the Hebrews, and you'll see that Christ makes his priestly offering not in an earthly temple—not in Jerusalem—but in the heavenly sanctuary. That's why the congregation launches every Mass's eucharistic prayer with the

Sanctus, the "Holy, Holy, Holy," which is the song of the angels in the heavenly liturgy, as we know from the book of Isaiah and the book of Revelation.

The priest then offers the longest prayer of the Mass, the eucharistic prayer. It contains elements of remembrance; it recalls the deeds of the Lord. It makes thanksgiving for these deeds; "thanksgiving" is the literal meaning of the Greek word *eucharistia,* from which we get our "Eucharist." But the heart of the eucharistic prayer is the Institution Narrative, the story of Jesus's priestly offering at the Last Supper, which was consummated on the cross at Calvary. The priest gives the narrative as we find it in the Gospels and Saint Paul's First Epistle to the Corinthians; and, when he speaks the words of Christ, he fulfills the command of Christ: *Do this in remembrance of me.*

In the eucharistic prayer, the most profound change takes place. The bread and wine truly become the Body and Blood of Jesus Christ. They're not symbols. They're his substance, and they contain infinity: Jesus's Body and Blood, soul and divinity.

The Fathers' testimonies to Jesus's Real Presence are abundant and they echo Jesus's own language at the Last Supper ("This is my body . . . my blood") and in the sixth chapter of John's Gospel. Ignatius the Apostolic Father many times called the Eucharist the "flesh" of Jesus[7] and the "blood of God."[8] Justin Martyr, shortly afterward, said that the Eucharist is "both the flesh and the blood of that incarnated Jesus."[9] The testimonies are just as powerful in Clement of Alexandria, Origen, Cyprian, Cyril of Jerusalem, Ambrose, Augustine, Chrysostom, Cyril of Alexandria, and so many others. Jesus's Real Presence in the Eucharist is among the most consistent and constant teachings of the early Church Fathers. To deny it is really to undermine

Christianity itself, as it has been known and practiced since the time of the apostles.

The early Christians strove to find language that could adequately serve the beauty of the eucharistic mystery. Saint Justin Martyr composed his description of the Mass around the year AD 150, and he could not find a word to describe the change, so he made up a verb! He said the elements were "eucharisted."[10] Egyptian authors writing in the late 100s and mid-200s used the verb "sanctified" to describe what happens during the eucharistic prayer. Saint Cyril of Jerusalem spoke of it as a "transformation." Saint Gregory of Nyssa said it was an "essential change" and "radical transformation."[11]

The word *transubstantiation* arose much later, in the Middle Ages, when the Church needed more precise language to address new objections. This is a fine example of theology's application of human reason, which is God-given, to a divine mystery that is beyond full description, like the incarnation itself.

The marvel of the Eucharist was prefigured in so many ways through the Old Testament: the bread and wine offered by the priest Melchizedek, the manna given by God in the desert, and the Bread of Presence offered in the Temple. When the Jerusalem priests brought the Showbread out of the sanctuary, they would hold it up before the people and cry out, "Behold, the face of God!" Wow—what was God preparing them for?

He was preparing them for the Eucharist that so many of us today take for granted!

In a similar way, our New Testament priests hold up the gifts for our adoration during the eucharistic prayer and afterward. In the Communion Rite that follows, we herald our Eucharist Lord repeatedly as "Lamb of God."

The more I meditate on this as an older man, the harder it is for me to hold myself together. I'm overwhelmed by joy, gratitude, and a sense of my own unworthiness. My spiritual father, Father Martin, once said to me: "When I pray the consecration at Mass, I can't think about it too much, or I couldn't do it." Even as someone with a nonspeaking part, I'm beginning to understand what he meant.

We pray the Lord's Prayer, as the Lord taught us, just as the early Christians prescribed in the *Didache*. We make our peace with one another and sign it with a handshake, just as we are instructed in the Gospel and in the *Didache*—so that our sacrifice may be pure.

And then Jesus is brought to us. He comes to us. And we receive him into our hearts as our personal Lord and Savior. We do it verbally when the priest says, "The Body of Christ," and we answer, "Amen!" But we even do it *physically*, by taking his Body and Blood into our own bodies. His Body is actually within our bodies! Yes, this is a spiritual experience. But it is also incarnational. It is enfleshed. That is why, after we receive him, it's so important for us to spend a few precious minutes in prayer, meditating on this awesome mystery and privilege.

Every Mass is an altar call. At every Mass the incarnation, birth, ministry, death, and resurrection of Jesus Christ—from eternity and for each of us personally—is sacramentally extended and re-presented out of love. We respond out of love.

At every Mass there is an altar call, and at every Mass we stand up for Jesus. And we do so much more than that. We mingle our substance with his. We partake of his divine nature, just as the Bible promises.

We stand up individually, but also collectively. We stand

together as a Church that's Catholic—universal—because we can't do much on our own. We need our brothers and sisters in the congregation to stand up with us, to lead us, to follow us, to support us if we fall, and to lean on us if they're falling.

The Mass is at once the corporate and the individual experience of the infinite and the eternal. We receive the Creator and the Redeemer—through the very things of creation. It is mystical.

If we truly believe all that we learn in mystagogy, how can we ever show up at Mass and just say the words in a rote manner?

Yet, alas, we do. Pope Francis, not long ago, warned us about being like "mummies in a museum."[12]

He's right to warn us, but it's not entirely a bad thing if we show up, now and then, when our brain is not up to the task, or when we're terribly distracted, or when we're feeling overwhelmed by the world. When I'm too tired to pray, I go and pray anyway. And it's great. I can lean back on the liturgy and know that it will carry me. It's God's work, and it doesn't depend on me. In the Mass we can abandon ourselves to the work of God and let ourselves be carried by the prayer of the people of God.

———

Mystagogy is a work the Fathers modeled for us, their children, and it is a work they passed on to us.

I have tried to contain the ocean in a thimble, and in that I have failed, but I hope you have acquired at least a taste for that divine salt. I hope it will never lose its savor for you.

Let every Mass be a personal and communal encounter with

Jesus Christ—an encounter that is personal, intimate, and profoundly life changing. That is my most heartfelt prayer for you and me.

I encourage you—and urge you—to go to the Fathers and search out their teachings on liturgy: Cyril of Jerusalem's *On the Mysteries,* Ambrose of Milan's *On the Sacraments.* Learn why Chrysostom could stay faithful to the Church's liturgical practice even though it needed reform, even though it pained him at times, even though he was not above complaining about it.

Chapter 8

NOTHING WITHOUT THE BISHOP

OMMUNION MAKES COMMUNITY, RIGHT? SAINT
Paul laid that down as a rule of Christian life: "Because there is one bread, we who are many are one body, for we all partake of the one bread" (1 Corinthians 10:17). The eucharistic prayer of the *Didache* reflects this belief: "Even as this broken bread was scattered over the hills, and was gathered together and became one, so let your Church be gathered together from the ends of the earth into your kingdom."[1] If we in our little flock at Alverna were simply faithful to this call, I thought, the details of our common life would fall into place.

I didn't expect it to be easy. I was willing to do hard labor in the Lord's vineyard. But as I moved from Indiana to Arkansas with my handful of companions, I had high expectations. Community life, I thought, should just descend like a New Jerusalem from the heavens into the Ozarks.

It didn't happen that way. We made our way by fits and starts, trial and error. The trial was constant. The errors were many. (And they continue to this day.) We had only the vaguest sense of discipline and order. I was reluctant to exercise authority. We tried to be democratic about everything, even the most basic domestic decisions, like groceries, and we experienced paralysis by process.

When I look back upon those times, I can still feel the unease and dissatisfaction that marked the daily life of our little flock of half a dozen souls.

We did one thing right, however, from the very beginning. We placed ourselves under the authority of the local bishop, Andrew McDonald of Little Rock.

At first Bishop Andrew was formal with us and somewhat distant. We were coming in from outside, after all, and looking and talking a little like hippies. What we were proposing didn't seem to fit neatly with the life of the Church as it was ordered in the twentieth century—though we were striving to be grounded in the tradition. We were operating under the cover of Franciscanism, but we had begun to include elements of other spiritualities from the Christian East and West. We had begun, as well, to integrate all states of life: celibate, married, and single. Bishop Andrew had to be cautious, and he was.

Over time, that changed. He became more of a friend and a father. I came to treasure his counsel and depend upon his wisdom.

He guided me in many practical matters as my companions and I took our first halting steps. It was he who helped me to recognize the leadership potential of one of our members.

Sister Viola Pratka had come to our young community after twenty-five years of consecrated life as a member of the Sisters of the Incarnate Word order. A prodigy in her religious development, she had entered the convent in her early teens. While still very young, she experienced the great benefits of the demanding discipline and deep culture of religious life. Through the sixties and seventies, though, her community caught something of the spirit of the age, and she felt she was increasingly out of step.

Given leave by her superiors, she found her way to us in Arkansas.

She had actually met me in Texas, when she was helping to organize my performance with the Dallas Symphony Orchestra. She was not particularly impressed by me, and she took my introversion for egotism. In spite of that, she got to know the community members, and she discerned a call to join us.

In her quiet way, she made an immediate difference. Viola drew from decades of experience in community life. We were flailing because of our inexperience. She drew also from the deep well of tradition, having been schooled at a time when the curriculum emphasized the riches of the Christian heritage. We were putting ourselves through remedial education to make up for the poor formation of our youth.

Her insights seemed to possess supernatural clarity at times, and perhaps they did.

She gently but enthusiastically guided us toward regularity and accountability in our cycles of work, prayer, and fasting. Because of her suggestion, we took up the early Church's practice of fasting twice a week, on Wednesday and Friday. And her knowledge was practical as well as spiritual. She helped us to see how we might operate our kitchen more economically, drawing on homey yet institutional lessons one could learn only in a convent of fifty nuns.

As much as the community took to her, Viola took to the community. She petitioned Rome for release from her vows. She asked, at the same time, for permanent admission to our community at Little Portion Hermitage.

Her guidance proved invaluable, then, as we emerged as a family with an identity, the Brothers and Sisters of Charity, and as we began—like Pachomius, Basil, and Benedict long before us—to draw up our rule of common life. It was Viola who urged me, as I composed our Rule, to "just write from the Scriptures."

In the first generation after the apostles, Saint Ignatius wrote emphatically: "Do nothing without the bishop."[2] Ignatius had learned the faith from the apostles and held himself, first, accountable to their authority and then accountable to their tradition, which is the memory of the Church. It was not to gather power for himself that Ignatius wrote those words. He was powerless at the time when he wrote them, traveling in chains under military escort, on his way to Rome for the execution of his death sentence. Ignatius, like Clement before him, was simply trying to preserve the apostolic order for the next generation. With the charisms of Pentecost had come the structure of the Church. With the descent of the Spirit had come the authority of the apostolic office.

The earliest Fathers saw that rebellious spirits would always challenge the authority of the apostles, which had been vested in the bishops. They saw, too, that worldly men would be attracted to the office for its prestige. Thus, they took pains to protect the office as it had been established by Christ and occupied by the apostles. Though they had limited time and means at their disposal, they devoted much of their efforts to elucidating the authority and ministry of the Catholic Church's clergy, especially of the bishop.

It soon became clear to me that God had sent Viola Pratka to be something more than a member of our community. Her insights were so profound; she seemed to speak with the voice of the Spirit. Her particular charism seemed more like my own, as founder, than like the gifts of other community members.

In prayer I sensed also that God was calling Viola and me to be united in marriage.

This was puzzling to me, as my own plan had been to live as a celibate for my remaining years. Marriage was not part of the story line as I had written it.

It wasn't that I faced any impediment. My marriage to Nancy had been annulled by the Church. The temporary private vows I had taken in Indiana had long expired. And Rome had released Viola from her obligations.

Marriage was not what I had willed for my life. Yet increasingly I felt that it was God's will.

Viola, too, had begun to discern the same unexpected vocation.

We were not inclined to trust our feelings, so we determined to make a pilgrimage and retreat. We would go back to Alverna, the community's earthly origin, and take counsel with Father Martin. Both of us were kind of hoping that he would raise a loud objection. We were happy as celibates. But that's not what happened.

Father Martin told us that there were no natural or supernatural impediments to our marrying, but that we should be prepared to face misunderstanding and gossip from those who would not accept that our intentions were pure, deliberate, and undertaken with deference to all due authority.

We were convinced by the end of our retreat that our union in marriage was God's will. On our return to Arkansas we consulted as well with Bishop Andrew, who assured us that there was no impediment to our marriage—though he, too, like Father Martin, warned us that we would be misunderstood. The bishop even commended us for actively seeking God's will rather than trying to gain the Church's consent for our own will. "You will rock the boat," he predicted. And rock the boat we did.

God joined us as husband and wife on February 17, 1989. Our dear Father in Christ Bishop Andrew presided at our wedding, witnessing our vows in the community's newly constructed Charity Chapel.

We have lived since then as husband and wife. Our hearts remain fully monastic, and our commitment is solidified through the sacrament of matrimony. In that we can be examples to celibates and married couples alike. To the community we are cofounders—father and mother—and the community has prospered as a family this way for a quarter century, as I write these words.

——

Family cohesion was the experience of the early Church. It's not that everything always went smoothly. It's not that every bishop was a telegenic domestic patriarch like we find on the prime-time sitcoms. But the Church was recognized as a Church because it gathered around men who were verifiable successors to the apostles.

Even before the canon of the New Testament was widely known, the lines of family authority were clearly in place. In the first century, Saint Clement said:

Christ is from God, and the Apostles are from Christ. Both therefore came of the will of God in the appointed order. . . . Preaching everywhere in country and town, they appointed their first fruits . . . to be bishops and deacons for those who should believe. . . .

They appointed these men, and afterward they provided a succession, so that if these should fall asleep, other approved men should succeed to their service.[3]

The apostles established rules for succession, Clement explained, because they knew (by supernatural grace) that there would be "strife for the office of bishop."[4]

Clement's contemporaries were careful to preserve this *hierarchy*, or sacred order. Clement valued *homonoia* in the Church more than any other quality. *Homonoia* is harmony, unity of mind and spirit.

Few writers in all of history have written as poetically about the office of bishop as Ignatius of Antioch. Hear him out.

It is proper for you to act together in harmony with the mind of the bishop, as you are already doing. For your presbytery, which is worthy of its name and worthy of God, is attuned to the bishop as strings to a harp. Therefore in your unanimity and harmonious love Jesus Christ is sung.[5]

Let us, therefore, be careful not to oppose the bishop, in order that we may be obedient to God.[6]

Ignatius compares the bishop to God the Father[7] and to Jesus.[8] He says it is the bishop who validates the Eucharist: "Let that be deemed a proper Eucharist which is administered either by the bishop, or by one to whom he has entrusted it."[9] Indeed, he says, without the three orders of clergy (bishop, presbyter, deacon), the Church does not exist.[10] Without submission to the bishop, the Gospel is not reliably passed on.[11] Without the unity that follows from submission, the Church decomposes and credibility is diminished. Ignatius issued a plea for unity in the face of challenges that threatened to destroy the beautiful order of the first churches of Jesus Christ.

Some modern scholars have tried to dismiss the witness of Ignatius's letters. They say that the great bishop of Antioch effectively "invented" the office of bishop.[12] But the letters themselves do not support that reading. Ignatius nowhere argues for the authority of the bishop. He simply presents it as a commonly accepted fact and a consequence of communion in Christ. He assumes that it is accepted in Ephesus as in Smyrna, in Tralles as in Philadelphia, in Magnesia as in Antioch. By the time he is setting words to paper, the office of bishop was a distinguishing mark of a Christian congregation. It was essential and self-evident.

During the generation of the Apostolic Fathers there was some fluidity in the titles of Church office and in the roles assigned to those titles. The *Didache*, for example, speaks of "prophets" in the Church who perform some of the roles fulfilled by the "presbyters" in Ignatius's letters. The Church was working out its doctrine in practice. It was developing. But no one—least of all a traditional, apostolic man like Ignatius—was inventing things for the Church or imposing novelties on the Christian people.

Ignatius was on his way to die for Christ. He had nothing

to gain by speaking a falsehood. He sought only to transmit the truth he had received from the apostles, and to make it understood in many different congregations in the catholic world and the Catholic Church.

From what we see in his writings, we have to conclude that the people, for their part, were receptive to the message. Again, he presents no arguments for his position. He simply assumes that they find in the New Testament the same offices that he found there: bishop, presbyter, and deacon (see, for example, Philippians 1:1; 1 Timothy 5:17; James 5:14-15; and 1 Timothy 3:1-13). Many of the Fathers saw that three-part structure foreshadowed as well in the Old Testament offices of high priest, priest, and Levite.

—

In the third century, when the Christian historian Eusebius set out to collect the archival records of the generations that had gone before him, he established clear criteria for which churches he would include. He was interested only in those that could trace "lines of succession from the holy apostles." Why? Because, he said, he wanted to transmit faith that was "not modern or strange, but . . . primitive, unique, and true."[13]

Saint Irenaeus, in the second century, often emphasized apostolic succession as the prerequisite for doctrinal authority. Only bishops, he believed, had the authority from Christ to interpret the Scriptures for the life of the Church.

How could Irenaeus say that with authority? Because he was a bishop himself, and he had learned this from no less a bishop than Polycarp of Smyrna. Irenaeus said: "Polycarp . . . was not only instructed by Apostles, and conversed with many who had seen Christ, but was also, by apostles in Asia, appointed bishop of the Church in Smyrna."[14]

In the time of Irenaeus there were wayward Christians who championed an extreme form of private interpretation. They called themselves Gnostics, or "Knowers." Against them, Irenaeus argued: "The true knowledge is the doctrine of the apostles, and the ancient organization of the Church throughout the whole world, and the manifestation of the body of Christ according to the succession of bishops."[15]

The pre-eminent example of this succession, according to Irenaeus—and later Eusebius, Athanasius, Jerome, and Augustine—is the Church of Rome. He proclaimed the Roman Church as

> the greatest and most ancient Church known to all, founded and organized at Rome by the two most glorious apostles, Peter and Paul—that Church which has the tradition and the faith with which comes down to us after having been announced to men by the apostles. For with this Church, because of its superior origin, all churches must agree, that is, all the faithful in the whole world. And it is in her that the faithful everywhere have maintained the apostolic tradition.[16]

The greatest Scripture scholar in the ancient world, Saint Jerome, went further still as he noted the biblical prerogatives of the Bishop of Rome. In addressing Pope Damasus I, he said, "I speak with the successor of the fisherman and disciple of the cross. Following none but Christ as my primate, I am united in communion with Your Beatitude—that is, with the chair of Peter. Upon that Rock I know the Church is built. Whosoever eats a lamb outside this house is profane. Whoever is not in Noah's ark will perish when the flood prevails."[17]

What was abundantly evident in Scripture and tradition I found confirmed in my experience. Bishop Andrew McDonald served me as a father in the Church until his retirement in the Jubilee Year 2000—after an epic twenty-eight years in episcopal ministry. After his retirement, he continued to minister in the Church, presiding at the altars, joyful and wise in Jesus Christ, until his death in 2014. People continued to benefit from his kindness, as I did and as my fledgling community did.

I grieved when Bishop Andrew retired and left Arkansas. But Jesus promised not to orphan his people, not to leave us fatherless in our Mother Church. In the ordinary course of the Church's life, Bishop Andrew was succeeded by Bishop J. Peter Sartain (2000–2006) and Bishop Anthony Taylor (since 2008).

Though I have faced many trials in my personal work, and I have felt many "growing pains" as our community has developed through the years, I have always been able to work with the confidence of a child of God. The reason is simple: because I have known God's Fatherhood through the ministry of the men he has appointed to father me in the Church. I have often found comfort in knowing I don't need to be the final authority in community life. I could always find support in my bishop, his canonical visitor, or my spiritual father. I would not trade this for anything in this world.

Down the years I have encountered many non-Catholic

intentional communities similar to ours; and their members and leaders have often confessed a bit of envy for our healthy relationship with our bishop and the pope. When they face the inevitable challenges that are a part of community life, they lack the built-in accountability that comes with the Church's structures of authority. As a result, both members and leaders sometimes feel alienated from one another and very much alone.

People outside the Catholic Church sometimes misunderstand the way we Catholics view authority. It's not power so much as service. Jesus told his apostles: "He who is greatest among you shall be your servant" (Matthew 23:11). The bishops are, above all, ministers and servants of the Gospel—servants of God's servants.

Like the apostles—and like any father in any family—they can be prideful, fearful, impetuous, rash, and hard to get along with. They are even free, like Judas, to betray Jesus and sell him down the river. God knows the human condition, and he chooses to work with such men anyway, just as he chose his apostles, and just as he called forth the Fathers of the early Church.

Most of the early Fathers were bishops. There are exceptions to that rule. Justin Martyr and Tertullian were probably laymen, and Jerome was a simple priest. Many of the Desert Fathers were nonordained solitaries. But most of the Fathers of the Church held the paternal office in the Church that Bishop Andrew held. We know their works today only because their people treasured them and preserved them lovingly.

I understand the dynamic. I know that as long as I live—and as long as my wife, Viola, lives—we will treasure the teaching of Bishop Andrew McDonald. I suspect that for as long as there are Brothers and Sisters of Charity on the face of the earth, they will look back to Bishop Andrew as a benefactor, patron, teacher, and guide—in short, a father.

This is what we learn simply by living in the Church of Jesus Christ. We learn to live in the family of God by practicing our love for our fathers in the Church. We learned such love from the ancient Fathers. May we pass it on, in turn, to our children.

Chapter 9

CHARITY

FROM THE BEGINNING, I WANTED OUR COMMU-
nity to practice an *active* charity. Through my years in
the Jesus Movement, I encountered people who seemed
to reduce evangelism to the distribution of tracts. If you got the
leaflet into someone's hand, your job was done. You did what
you could. If you were really on fire, maybe you'd walk folks the
extra steps to say the Sinner's Prayer.

I felt that the Brothers and Sisters of Charity—by our very
name—had a more demanding vocation. This was confirmed by
my reading of the Scriptures.

> If a brother or sister is ill-clad and in lack of daily food,
> and one of you says to them, "Go in peace, be warmed and
> filled," without giving them the things needed for the body,
> what does it profit? So faith by itself, if it has no works, is
> dead. But some one will say, "You have faith and I have
> works." Show me your faith apart from your works, and I by
> my works will show you my faith. You believe that God is
> one; you do well. Even the demons believe—and shudder.
> Do you want to be shown, you shallow man, that faith apart
> from works is barren? (James 2:15-20)

Those are bracing words, and they are true marks of biblical religion. The Old Testament prophets repeatedly declared the wrath of God upon those who neglected or exploited the poor (see, for example, Amos 2:6-7).

The early Church imitated Christ, whom the Father "anointed . . . to preach good news to the poor . . . to proclaim release to the captives . . . to set at liberty those who are oppressed" (Luke 4:18). Jesus didn't just use words for his proclamation. He backed his words up with saving deeds. He fed people. He healed them. He set them free when a mob wanted to stone them. He looked after widows and restored their livelihood.

So the Church, too, healed in Jesus's name, established full-time ministries of service to the poor, and took up collections for both local and global relief (see Acts 6:1-3; Romans 15:26; 1 Corinthians 16:1; 2 Corinthians 9:1).

Tertullian said that the Christians of his time (in the second century) wore charity like a brand on their bodies. Slaves were marked with a brand that showed the identity of their owner. Charity was the mark that distinguished Christians from others.

Charity was a radical new idea in the Greco-Roman world. It was common for wealthy people to make ostentatious acts of *philanthropy*—building a sports arena, paving a road, or sponsoring a yearly distribution of meat and bread. But it was done not for God's glory, or even the gods' glory, but for the fame of the benefactor and his family. Even the pagan temples bore gigantic inscriptions giving credit to their sugar daddies.

But the Christian way was different. Tertullian spelled it out: "to support and bury poor people, to supply the wants of orphans, and elderly people who are homebound, those who have suffered shipwreck, and those who have been condemned to work in the mines, or banished to the islands, or shut up in prisons."[1] There was no earthly glory in these works. There was probably little gratitude; human nature had not (and has not) changed since those nine ex-lepers left without thanking Jesus (see Luke 17:17-18).

That didn't matter. Christians fed, clothed, healed, and comforted other people because they loved Christ, their King, and he had said to them: "as you did it to one of the least of these my brethren, you did it to me" (Matthew 25:40).

Our path, then, was clear to us, and we acted locally, in our Arkansas community, from the start. Very early in our community life, we developed a special relationship with Mercy Corps, a worldwide faith-based relief service founded by my friend Dan O'Neill. Mercy Corps' mission is to alleviate suffering, poverty, and oppression by helping people to build just, secure, and productive communities.

We also sent members to practice a ministry of presence among the poor in Central America, providing basic health care, counsel, catechesis, transportation, and other basic services—providing friendship, really: the friendship of Jesus Christ.

The identifying mark of the Brothers and Sisters of Charity—our "brand," to use Tertullian's term—should always be the self-giving, life-giving love of Jesus. It must always be charity.

———

Charity was not something incidental to the life of the early Church. It was not a special program. Care for the poor was at the heart of the Church's faith. It was inseparable from the

Church's sacramental life. It was the Christian vocation. In Scripture the Greek word *leitourgia* is applied not only to worship and ministry, but also to care for the poor in the Church (see 2 Corinthians 9:11-12).

I mentioned, in an earlier chapter, that Justin Martyr's and Tertullian's accounts of Christian charity take place in the context of their descriptions of the Mass. They mention the offertory collection, and then they speak of its distribution.

Justin and Tertullian wrote their apologetic works very early in the Church's history, the mid- to late second century. But long before their time we find the same connection between charity and the sacraments in the letters of Ignatius of Antioch. Ignatius made the connection explicit. He said that the mark of heretics—their "brand," so to speak—was twofold: neglect of the poor and denial of Jesus's Real Presence in the Eucharist.

> Consider how contrary to the mind of God are the heretics in regard to the grace of Jesus Christ that has come to us. They have no concern for charity, none for the widow, the orphan, the oppressed, none for the man in prison, the hungry or the thirsty. They abstain from the Eucharist and from prayer, because they do not admit that the Eucharist is the flesh of our Savior Jesus Christ, flesh that suffered for our sins and that the Father, in his graciousness, raised from the dead.[2]

For Ignatius the connection is very clear. If the heretics did not recognize the flesh of Jesus in the holy sacrament, they would not recognize it in the flesh of the poor and oppressed.

This connection, between sacramentality and mercy, is pervasive in the works of the Fathers. A third-century manual of Church discipline, a close kin of the *Didache*, instructs the faithful: "Widows and orphans are to be revered like the altar."[3] Such a command envisions Christian social life as a network of charity, but it presumes a deep sacramental piety.

For John Chrysostom, those two elements—charity for the poor and sacramental piety—are interdependent and inseparable.

> Do you wish to honor the body of Christ? Do not ignore him when he is naked. Do not pay him homage in the temple clad in silk only then to neglect him outside where he suffers cold and nakedness. He who said: "This is my body" is the same One who said: "You saw me hungry and you gave me no food" and "Whatever you did to the least of my brothers you did also to me." . . . What good is it if the Eucharistic table is overloaded with golden chalices, when he is dying of hunger? Start by satisfying his hunger, and then with what is left you may adorn the altar as well.[4]

We moderns have come to equate charity with philanthropy. We have come to see it almost exclusively in terms of the public acts of do-gooders. But the ancients had a much more robust view, based on the sacrament of Christ's flesh received in the Eucharist, based on the sacrament of divine life received in baptism.

As he instituted the Eucharist, Jesus took bread, blessed it, and declared it to be his body. Yet he revealed to Saul the persecutor that the Church, too, in some mysterious way was also his body. "Saul, Saul," he said, "why do you persecute me?" (Acts 9:4). Christians were not merely his people, or his followers, or his disciples, or even his family. They were all those things, but their primary identification was deeper still. They were his body. "The bread which we break," Paul wrote to the Corinthians, "is it not a participation [communion] in the body of Christ? Because there is one bread, we who are many are one body, for we all partake of the one bread" (1 Corinthians 10:16-17). Later in the same letter he said:

> For just as the body is one and has many members, and all the members of the body, though many, are one body, so it is with Christ. For by one Spirit we were all baptized into one body—Jews or Greeks, slaves or free—and all were made to drink of one Spirit. For the body does not consist of one member but of many. . . . Now you are the body of Christ and individually members of it. (1 Corinthians 12:12-14, 27)

In the Eucharist, Jesus gives the Church his body; and through the Eucharist the Church knows *communion with* his body, and *communion in* his body. Believers are united with Jesus and with one another. Their mission, moreover, is not self-enclosed; Jesus sent the apostles to all the world (Acts 1:8). Thus, every nonbeliever is a potential believer—a potential member of the Body of Christ. Christian charity, therefore, is necessarily indiscriminate and universal. Christians imitate God, whose rain falls on the just and unjust. Christians are required to love even their enemies (Matthew 5:44).

It is interesting to note that such outgoing charity became the hallmark even of Christians who sought *separation* from the world. The earliest communities of ascetics found ways to be of service. The accounts of the Desert Fathers are replete with examples of heroic charity—monks leaving aside their ordinary tasks to carry those who were hobbled, or to build shelters for the homeless and abandoned. Their self-giving was often heroic. In the first years of the fifth century, Abba Agathon said: "If I could meet a leper, give him my body and take his, I should be very happy." The monk who recorded that saying commented: "That indeed is perfect charity."[5]

Over time, such self-giving became habitual; and, when the persecutions ceased, charity took remarkable institutional forms. The monasteries became the birthplace of "public"—that is, publicly available—education and health care. Every monastery was expected to have a charitable outreach. The monks took it upon themselves to learn to provide medical care and practice pharmacology. The monks in Egypt developed a prodigious knowledge of medicinal plants. They recorded traditional folk remedies for coughs and colds, eye complaints, colic, diarrhea, constipation—whatever ailed their neighbors. Today, in the twenty-first century, major pharmaceutical companies have funded researchers to go back into those ancient monastic texts in search of possible cures.

Whether the drug companies find anything useful is immaterial (literally). The important thing is the *charity* of the monks, who devoted so much of their lives to caring for their neighbors, risking exposure to disease, and taking pains to pass their wisdom on to future generations. This sort of medical care was a Christian innovation, a product of divine charity, a manifestation of eucharistic grace. The world had never known anything so glorious.

—

All the great social reformers of the early Church were also great liturgical reformers. Look into the lives of and liturgies bearing the names of Basil of Caesarea, John Chrysostom, and Gregory the Great, to name just three prominent examples. They sought to strengthen the bond of community by renewing communal worship—renewing the sense of the sacred, the doctrine of the sacraments, and the power of the biblical proclamation. The liturgy was a powerful medium for the Scriptures' consistent summons to justice and responsibility.

Basil's reform was holistic. His charitable works were so extensive that they formed a "New City." That's what the locals called it. It was a city of charity, where streets were lined with hospices, hospitals, travelers' hostels, trade schools, and soup kitchens. All of these were staffed by the ascetics who lived in Basil's community—the very monks and nuns who carried out his liturgical reform, chanting their Divine Office of psalms by day and by night.

Christians were called to render to God the things that are God's. Everything in the world belonged to God, and was owed to him, and could be returned to him in the person of "the least" in any community.

For the Gentiles—the Greeks and Romans who had not known the Hebrew prophets—this represented a radically new order of justice in the world. Who were the least in their world? The newborn, the preborn, the people on crutches and using canes, the people whose diseases were contagious and incurable, the people who had been publicly shamed for some reason. These people didn't matter. They could be treated with contempt. Some of them could be legally killed. Consider that there were no laws against sexually abusing slaves—until Christians made laws.

The Church of the Fathers—the Church of Jesus Christ— made room for everyone. The Fathers were *fathers* to the most vulnerable groups at the margins of Greco-Roman society. They spoke out consistently as their defenders.

"Whatever you do to the least of these, you do also to me" (Matthew 25:45). The invisible poor were visible to the Church of Christ, because they *were* Christ to the Church. That's why the Fathers condemned abortion, euthanasia, capital punishment, and indiscriminate acts of war. Christians who committed these sins were excommunicated automatically, and reconciled only after penance.

Even the emperor Theodosius was subject to this severe mercy; he was publicly denounced by Ambrose of Milan and barred from Communion till he had made reparation for the slaughter of his enemies. His retributive violence ran contrary to the charity that should "brand" the life of a Christian. His actions rendered him unfit for Holy Communion.

In recent years, God has sent the Church a pope after the heart of the great Fathers. Pope Francis, from the day of his inauguration, has preached Good News to the poor, has called the powerful to render mercy and justice, and has brought together the wrathful to pray for peace.

He issues his call not just to leaders of nations, but to leaders of households and mid-level managers in small corporations, to argumentative siblings and feuding neighbors, to competing political candidates and owners of rival businesses.

Are you Christian? Do you wear charity as a brand upon your body?

There is nothing new about the questions Pope Francis uses to confront the complacent. They shook up the old world and made it into a New City. May they shake up our world. And may they shake up me and my community, and you and yours.

Chapter 10

STEWARDSHIP OF THE EARTH

WHEN I SPEAK OF THE FATHERS' WITNESS TO Christian social doctrine, or their witness to the Real Presence, or even their use of holy water, I am walking a well-worn path. To speak of the Fathers' "ecological" concern is quite another matter. The word has become a worn coin for us. It's often shorthand for a rather vast complex of scientific research and political positions. Under the "ecological" umbrella, you'll find passionate advocacy of policies and activities, ranging from litter cleanup to population control.

There are certainly a multitude of Old and New Testament passages that connect the sinful greed of a people to natural disasters. God often uses the natural world to stir people to return to the right path. In recent years, theologians and popes—most notably Benedict XVI—have begun to address ecology in a very urgent way.

But the Fathers did not know the word. It's a modern coinage from ancient Greek roots, meaning, roughly, wisdom (*logos*) about the household (*oikos*). The Fathers were unaware, as far as we can tell, of the issues that seem so urgent to many people today—climate change, population density, or the long-term effects of pollution on ecosystems. I want to respect their silence, and I do not intend to play ventriloquist across the centuries.

I do believe, however, that the Fathers' moral and ascetical principles are more than applicable to modern circumstances. I'll go further still and say that if Christians had followed the teachings of the Fathers, maybe we wouldn't be facing some of the environmental and social crises we face today.[1]

The truth is that, except in times of famine, the ancient Fathers showed little sense of the scarcity of natural resources. Even then, they looked upon the situation as a temporary trial—an opportunity given to the rich to detach themselves from the possessions that could hinder their spiritual lives. Basil the Great and his sometime best friend Gregory of Nazianzus argued that the most enlightened self-interest consisted in sharing one's goods. In relieving the misfortunes of others, Gregory said, we "attend to our own interests." Thus, even self-regard is satisfied by charitable giving rather than by hoarding! Gregory concluded: "This to me is the most wonderful achievement of all, the short road to salvation, and the easiest ascent to heaven."[2] We can begin living a heavenly life on earth by making earth more godly.

For this we need to simplify; and simple living, I believe, is the truly identifiable prescription of the Fathers for the ailments of modern society and our old earth.

Jesus invited all Christians to live poverty. He called the poor blessed (Luke 6:20) and counseled his followers to be "poor in spirit" (Matthew 5:3). He warned us against hoarding possessions (Luke 12:16-21). And he urged his disciples, rather, to imitate the birds of the air, as they "neither sow nor reap nor gather into barns" (Matthew 6:26).

Jesus's call was not a summons to live in squalor and silent suffering. He evoked, rather, a life spontaneous, detached from earthly things, and thus always free to attach itself to God.

———

Indeed the teachings of the Fathers were helpful to us as we formed our first rules for common life at Little Portion Hermitage. My companions and I were much taken by the ascetical counsel of the Desert Fathers and the later adaptation of those counsels for urban monasteries.

We realized early on, however, that the ancient rules could not simply be applied to a community that included both families and solitaries. Our community represented a development, and (like Robert Frost) we wanted to find "an old-fashioned way to be new." We would have to find our own way of living poverty and sharing life in common while retaining private property and holding one another accountable for the modesty of our households. As we drafted our community rule, we strove to articulate general principles as well as practical applications.

Keeping in mind the legitimate needs of the family unit, simplicity and moderation are maintained even in the home, both as an environmental aid to nurturing interior poverty, and as an external manifestation to others of that interior poverty. Every home is called to reflect the peace of God through neatness and order, establishing a sacred space which manifests the fruits of the Spirit.[3]

Our goal has always been to observe a voluntary poverty and a voluntary community of goods. We strive for equality among members, but, again, this is achieved mostly in the way we choose to share with one another.

It helps us to go back, again and again, to the preaching of the Fathers—because that is precisely the life they urged on their communities, a life modeled in the Acts of the Apostles, where "all who believed were together and had all things in common; and they sold their possessions and goods and distributed them to all, as any had need" (Acts 2:44-45).

The Fathers wanted their congregations to simplify and declutter their lives. This was, for them, part of the process of redemption. In the beginning, God had made the world and declared it to be good. Sin introduced disorder into his creation. Salvation through Jesus, then, represented a recapitulation—a return to the beginning, a new creation (2 Corinthians 5:17; Galatians 6:15; Revelation 21:1).

As God is refashioning the earth, he is healing our souls and our bodies. And as he is healing us, he is refashioning the earth. The Fathers urged Christians to be willing participants in the process. God created the world without us, and we wounded his creation; he will save the world we wounded, but only if we participate in the healing.

As I said at the beginning of this chapter, none of the Fathers presents a sustained moral reflection on what we would today call "environmentalism" or "ecology." Nevertheless, the Fathers gave us excellent biblical principles for understanding our own situation, and these, I believe, can be enormously helpful for the practical application of what we have learned from modern science. Many devout Christians are eager to formulate an "eco-theology" and a morality of environmental responsibility. These are praiseworthy endeavors, and we can move forward all the more surely when we also look backward to the tradition.

In the pages that follow I intend to outline just a few of the Fathers' observations about creation and their counsels for simple living. I have no desire to alter the direction of future theology. I do wish, however, to meditate, at least for a moment, on the necessary foundations for my own efforts at living simply and living in tune with nature; I pray, of course, that readers will also find these meditations helpful.

1. The world is good. This may seem like a no-brainer. It is, after all, the clear teaching of the first chapter of the Bible, where God repeatedly looks at his creation, and declares it to be "good." Christians and Jews have always believed that the world is fundamentally good, and its goodness is marred only by human sin.

Jesus himself came to overcome the damage done on earth by sin. He came "to reconcile to himself all things, whether on earth or in heaven, making peace by the blood of his cross" (Colossians 1:20). Again we see that God loved the world, to the point of completely giving himself for its sake.

Yet this view of creation—as good and redeemed—was not the norm in ancient societies. Many pagan philosophers looked at the pervasiveness of suffering and decay—and the universality of death—and concluded that the world was a bad place. Some believed that the material world was a prison for spiritual beings (like you and me), who were trapped in bodies by a tyrannical demigod. Even some Christians fell for this way of thinking, and their heresies sometimes threatened the churches where the Fathers presided. This was true already in the apostolic generation, when Saint Paul found it necessary to condemn those who would forbid the enjoyment of created goods (1 Timothy 4:3). In the centuries that followed, the Gnostics systematized these strange ideas, and, later, the Manicheans developed a corresponding ascetical method—and effective methods of making converts.

The Gnostics took certain Scriptures that spoke in a negative way about "the world," and they made these absolute. Meanwhile, they neglected the fact that "God so loved the world" that he sent his only Son to save it.

The world is indeed fallen; and its disorder does indeed drag the spirit down with it. It is wounded, but still good. God made it that way; and Jesus came to re-establish its original integrity through his birth into it, and his life, death, and resurrection.

2. There is a God-given order to creation; it can be discerned and it should be respected. Saint Paul knew this: "Ever since the creation of the world his invisible nature, namely, his eternal power and deity, has been clearly perceived in the things that have been made" (Romans 1:20). This has always been the way of biblical religion:

> *And if men were amazed at their power and working,*
> *let them perceive from them*

how much more powerful is he who formed them.
For from the greatness and beauty of created things
comes a corresponding perception of their Creator.
   (Wisdom 13:4–5)

For the early Fathers, as for Saint Paul and the Book of Wisdom, the order observed in the cosmos implied a corresponding order for human behavior. Saint Clement of Rome observed the harmony in the skies and seas, and he proposed it as a model for harmony within the Church.

> The heavens, revolving under his government, are subject to him in peace. Day and night run the course appointed by him, in no way hindering each other. The sun and moon, with the companies of the stars, roll on in harmony according to his command, within their prescribed limits, and without any deviation. The fruitful earth, according to his will, brings forth food in abundance, at the proper seasons, for man and beast and all the living beings upon it, never hesitating, nor changing any of the ordinances which he has fixed.[4]

Basil the Great looked at the order of creation and saw it as a revelation of the Creator. He saw "heaven and earth, the vast deep and living creatures that move in the waters, animals of the dry land, and plants, stars, air, seasons," and he called them "manifold evidence of design."[5]

If God established an order, it is good for Christians to observe it, understand it, describe it, and respect it. Such respect represents the original impulse toward an environmental ethic.

The historian of science Stanley Jaki argued that it was also a necessary condition for the eventual establishment of scientific method.[6]

3. Human beings are the stewards (monarchs) of creation. Scripture places man and woman at the center of the creation narrative. Of all creatures, only man and woman were made in the image and likeness of God (Genesis 1:26). God, moreover, gave them the fruits of the earth for their use, and all the animals for their mastery (1:28). He deeded the world to man "to till it and to keep it" (Genesis 2:15). It was man who gave names to all the creatures (Genesis 2:19).

God made all the earth to provide sustenance for and to delight the human race. Why are there rivers and waterfalls? Because, say the Fathers, human beings get thirsty, and they like to go for a swim now and then. In the first century, Saint Clement of Rome declared: "The ever-flowing fountains were formed both for enjoyment and health; they furnish without fail their breasts *for the life of men.*"[7]

God gave humankind dominion over his vast creation. He gave Adam a share in divine kingship. Saint Gregory of Nyssa taught: "God made man capable of carrying out his role as king of the earth. . . . Man was created in the image of the One who governs the universe. Everything demonstrates that from the beginning his nature was marked by royalty. . . . He is the living image who participates by his dignity in the perfection of the divine archetype."[8]

The Fathers saw human beings as the responsible guardians of creation. I must admit that at times I am tempted to see fallen humanity as a blight on creation. Nevertheless, it should go without saying that any kind of antihuman environmentalism would be alien (and anathema) to our Christian ancestors, as would any kind of ecological doctrine that denied the special dignity of the human race. Humanity, for the Fathers, was not just another variety of meat in the food chain. The human race is the reason for creation. Creation is an expression of God's love for us. Ours is the nature he assumed for himself in saving the world.

Yet with great power he bestowed great responsibility. As Pope Saint John Paul II explained: "Man's lordship however is not absolute, but ministerial: it is a real reflection of the unique and infinite lordship of God. Hence man must exercise it with wisdom and love, sharing in the boundless wisdom and love of God."[9] Our stewardship is no license to abuse creation. We are to care for creation through the power God has given us as guardians.

As time goes on, the traditional scientific means of defining the uniqueness of the human being—the use of tools or language, for example—are proving more difficult to defend. But the utter uniqueness of the human being remains self-evident. After all, what other creature can have such a negative, or potentially positive, impact on the entire planet?

4. Sin creates environmental havoc. That is evident from the book of Genesis. Immediately after the original sin, Adam finds himself out of sync with the ground. It rebels against his efforts (Genesis 3:17-19). He plants food, and it comes up weeds—thorns and thistles. The ground itself is accursed because Adam has failed in his stewardship. The same cosmic principles are evident in the curses of Deuteronomy, chapter 28, where the world itself seems to rise in rebellion against its sinful guardians.

Basil and Chrysostom saw the same dynamic at work in their own centuries. They assured the wealthy and powerful that their irresponsibility—their exploitation of the poor and their manipulation of markets—would bring a curse upon their own lives and their families, just as Adam's sin had consequences for his lands and for all his descendants.

Bad morals, say the Fathers, are bad for business in the long run. In the short run, they make for a miserable life, even amid comforts.

5. Christ came to heal creation. That is the lesson to be learned from the miracles in the Gospels. Blindness, paralysis, dropsy, hemorrhaging—these are all disorders, departures from God's original intention in creation. Jesus's earthly miracles were only the beginning. At the consummation, the Bible tells us, "he will wipe away every tear . . . and death shall be no more, neither shall there be mourning nor crying nor pain any more" (Revelation 21:4). "There shall no more be anything accursed" (Revelation 22:3).

In the meantime, Christians continue the healing work of Christ, restoring creation, as they can with God's help, to its original goodness. "For the creation waits with eager longing for the revealing of the children of God" (Romans 8:19).

The principles seem clear from Scripture and from the Fathers. What is it, then, that keeps us from exercising our stewardship as we should?

The universal disorder, it seems, has affected our desires and our wills, and we must seek healing for these. And the only proven cure is the ancient path, the ascetical way that was blazed by John the Baptist and Jesus.

That was the way of the Fathers of the Church. They detached themselves from the things of this world—so that they could give themselves entirely to God. They fasted—so that they would not be tempted to betray Jesus in order to avoid hunger. They went homeless, so that they would never fear exile. They counted comfort as nothing, so that they would not fear prison. They died to self, so that they would always be ready to embrace martyrdom, if that should prove to be their vocation. They went further in asceticism than their pre-Christian or heretical counterparts, but never to the point of denying the essential goodness of creation, the flesh, or things as basic as marriage and the domestic family.

In their detachment from creation, they gained perspective on it. They could see it in its true glory, and they could praise God for it. At the same time, they avoided the pitfalls of fearing it or lusting after it. The rigorist cults feared the world. The sensualists lusted after it. Christians loved it rightly, and in right order, after its Creator and as reflection of the Creator's glory.

The Fathers saw the absurdity of desiring to possess creation. Basil satirized human greed. "Why do you find gold so alluring?" he asked. "Gold is, after all, just a kind of mineral. . . . Tell me what benefit you gain by waving around a hand resplendent with gems? Shouldn't you blush instead for shame, having given in to a strange desire for pebbles, like the cravings of a pregnant woman?"[10]

Chrysostom noted that ownership is an illusion—or rather a trap, because possessions come to own their owner. If a family owns a hoard of gold, they need to buy locks for the doors of their home. They need to hire guards and build walls. They cannot go about as they wish, for fear of robbers and kidnappers. They are constantly besieged by relatives in need, by flatterers and by con men. Their wealth comes to direct or restrict their every movement.

"What ails you people?" Basil asked. "Who twisted the things that are yours into a plot against you?"[11]

On the other hand, Chrysostom said, "he who has nothing can possess everything."[12] A poor man can look out on a beautiful valley, knowing that he has no chance of owning the land, and he can simply enjoy its beauty, praising God. A man of great wealth might look at the same vista and be seized by the desire to possess it, planning the negotiations already in his mind. The vista will make the one man happy. The greed will make the other man miserable. For even if the rich man gets his piece of land, it cannot satisfy him.

Nothing can. All creation would not be enough, because it is not designed for that purpose. God made the things of this world to lead us to him in praise and thanksgiving. If we make them ends in themselves, we make them idols. If we prefer anything to Christ, we have already made it a god. If our lives are driven by acquisition and possession—if we become habitual collectors and hoarders—we are the most wretched and pitiable people on the planet, because we'll never be satisfied. Basil described one classic case: "He was made miserable by abundance, wretched by the good things he still expected to receive. The land does not produce revenue for him, but rather brings forth sighs of discontent."[13]

This is the stuff of many a midlife crisis, many a bout of existential dread, many a late night spent staring at the ceiling. Read the homilies of the early Fathers.[14] They were experts on the psychology of desire and ownership. And the attitudes they describe are even more relevant today, when many whom we call "poor" live amid more luxury than did the wealthy of the ancient world. The kings in the second century did not have air-conditioning, pills for pain relief, antibiotics, or access to high-speed transportation. Even the noble families could not count on safe drinking water. Poverty is a relative term.

And the Fathers recognized that poverty in itself is not a virtue. The conditions of poverty, like the conditions of wealth, can come to preoccupy the mind, distracting us from prayer. Poverty, like riches, can keep us from God.

What we want to acquire is neither wealth nor destitution—but rather detachment and simplicity, keeping only what we need, focusing without distraction on the one needful thing (Luke 10:42).

If such an attitude directs our consumption, the problem of pollution will take care of itself. The world can bear the weight of all of us when we all realize we need not claim ownership of the world.

Christians should be the first to recognize this—and they should be the pre-eminent models for living a simple life. Is that the case? Is this a word we hear preached from our pulpits? I'm not talking about policy here. I'm not talking about political or ideological advocacy. I'm not talking about Green sloganeering.

I'm talking about conversion of individual lives, families, and households.

—

At Little Portion we have long striven to live by this ancient way, and it has proven attractive to others. Early on in our history, people would beat a path to our door to find out how we do it—live close to the land, honor nature, establish relationships with local growers, do our own manual labor, and raise our own crops and livestock when possible. Periodically we have sponsored a School of Simple Living, to make a map so that modern families can travel the ancient path, the ascetical way.

Should we really need a school for this? Perhaps. But what we need more is a searching examination of conscience. That's where the Fathers will lead us in prayer. Are we the stewards God wants us to be?

Chapter 11

HEART AND HANDS AND VOICES

I F YOU BELONG TO A FAMILY, YOU HAVE DOCUMENTS that you consider somewhat definitive. They define you in a way. Your identity is wrapped up in them. My parents kept a strongbox with their marriage license and our birth certificates in it, along with our insurance policies.

The family I founded, the Brothers and Sisters of Charity, also has its defining documents.

Like most intentional Catholic communities, we have our Constitution and Rule. In addition to those big texts, we have the books I've written and the songs I've recorded. Their words help define our common life as a family.

We also have a few precious documents that didn't get burned up in the 2008 fire.

As we recovered from the fire, we came to a deeper appreciation of the importance of documents in our life. For months afterward, we would stand up to check records, only to remember that the records were no longer there.

Through loss we also learned that their value is relative. Documents are an important part of our life, but they're not the most important part. Our life includes our paperwork, but it's not reducible to it. The fire took our texts away, but not our common life—not our customs, habits, hierarchy, routines, rituals, and deeply ingrained ways of relating to one another.

What defines us more than our documents is that common life—which we pass on just by living it. What defines us most is our *tradition*. It is a *living* tradition!

Jesus warns against those merely *human* traditions that can lead people away from the word of God (see Matthew 15:5-6). But the New Testament confirms the importance of *sacred* tradition. Before the New Testament books were written, the Church was already living its life, and its life included rituals—anointing, absolving, ablutions, vows, and a council. Nowhere does the New Testament instruct future generations about how these things should be done. The sacred authors simply assumed that the life of the Church would always continue as it had before the Gospels and epistles were written. Indeed, it would be centuries before those texts were officially compiled—and still more centuries before the holy books were easily acquired.

Tradition is simply the act of "handing on," and the apostles were much concerned about it. The first Christians didn't have a New Testament yet, so they "devoted themselves to the apostles' teaching" (Acts 2:42). Paul said emphatically and repeatedly:

Maintain the traditions even as I have delivered them to you. (1 Corinthians 11:2)

So then, brethren, stand firm and hold to the traditions which you were taught by us, either by word of mouth or by letter. (2 Thessalonians 2:15)

> Now we command you, brethren, in the name of our Lord
> Jesus Christ, that you keep away from any brother who is
> living in idleness and not in accord with the tradition that
> you received from us. (2 Thessalonians 3:6)

In the tradition, the common life of the Church, the Holy
Spirit conserved the sacred texts, the sacred rites, the sense of
the sacred, and the sacred path—the way of living a Christian
life, in all its glory and in all its gritty detail.

The apostles handed it on, and they exhorted their congregations to "hold" it. It was something given in trust, but something that must be "held" in hand, and not simply stored away
in an attic. Tradition was to be lived. It was the Christian way
of family life.

—

When I say that our way of life has been conserved in the
Church, I don't mean to say it's indistinguishable from what it
was at the time of the Church Fathers. In essence, nothing has
changed. All the essentials are still in place. Our life, however,
has developed.

Development was necessary, and it's still necessary today. As
the faith spread out from Palestine, Christians had to render
the Good News in different languages, different idioms, and
different cultures. The act of translation required, first, an act
of reflection on what is essential—and then a search for near
equivalents. Every translation is an accommodation. Cynics say
that every translator is a traitor. But in Christian history that
has not been the case. The practice of the faith has spread widely

and manifested itself in a beautiful paisley pattern of spiritualities and devotions. It looks chaotic from up close, but there is a sense to it. There is a pattern, and there is a profound unity.

Nothing in the stunning diversity of Christian life marks a betrayal when it is carried on faithfully within the sacred tradition, within the Church of Jesus Christ, and obedient to the apostles and their successors. The Church is enriched by such development, and the Church guards development from lapsing into degeneration.

The faith does not change, though our understanding of it must necessarily develop. The early Church Fathers knew this. Saint Basil the Great explained:

> I consider that also in me the same doctrine has been developed through progress, and what now is mine has not taken the place of what existed in the beginning. . . . Through progress we observe a certain amplification of what we say, which is not a change from worse to better, but is a completing of that which was lacking, according to the increment of our knowledge.[1]

The Church, like an individual, comes to a deeper understanding of itself as time goes on. The baby is not the adult, but the adult is the same person as the baby. The great patristic scholar Blessed John Henry Newman noted that a stream meets many obstacles along its course, and appears different at each point, but the water remains the same.

The Church learns through the experience of reality. We cannot change the revelation we have received—in Scripture or in tradition—but we must grow in our understanding of it.

The age of the Fathers was a time of great turmoil, and it demanded a corresponding development in teaching. How should the Church go about reconciling and re-admitting sinners? Should the Church require apostates—those who have denied the faith—to be rebaptized? At what point should a scandalous sinner be called out and publicly excommunicated? Which Christian books were sacred and thus worthy of proclamation in public worship?

The Fathers had to confront these challenges and find answers. It was always an urgent matter, and they had to call councils, conduct in-depth studies, and discuss and debate each matter in light of the doctrine and practice of previous generations. They held themselves accountable to Christ, who was alive in their Church—and who had always been alive in their Church. Neither Scripture nor tradition nor the bishops' authority (the magisterium) represented the last word in the Church. In the time of the Fathers, it was always Jesus, and so it remains in the Church of the Fathers, even today.

Doctrine develops, but it does not change the Body of Christ. An acorn becomes a seedling, a sapling, and then an oak, but it will never become a pine. The Church grows in self-awareness. The Church reaches new peoples. The Church responds to circumstances unimagined in ancient times—like nuclear arms, capitalism, communism, organ transplantation, and cloning—but the Church of Jesus Christ does not change, because it is the Body of Christ, and he is the same yesterday, today, and forever (Hebrews 13:8).

Tradition is the memory of the Church, and the Church remembers Jesus, not as a figure of history, but as a man fully alive. For the Church is faithful to the command he gave for his remembrance. The memory of the Church is more than an instant replay. It is a re-presentation of a reality that's eternal. It is a Real Presence.

Even in the development of doctrine—no, *especially* in the development of doctrine—the Fathers were faithful to the Scriptures, which witness to the process.

> And his gifts were that some should be apostles, some prophets, some evangelists, some pastors and teachers, to equip the saints for the work of ministry, for building up the body of Christ, until we all attain to the unity of the faith and of the knowledge of the Son of God, to mature manhood, to the measure of the stature of the fullness of Christ; so that we may no longer be children, tossed to and fro and carried about with every wind of doctrine, by the cunning of men, by their craftiness in deceitful wiles. Rather, speaking the truth in love, we are to grow up in every way into him who is the head, into Christ, from whom the whole body, joined and knit together by every joint with which it is supplied, when each part is working properly, makes bodily growth and upbuilds itself in love. (Ephesians 4:11-16)

Development is not evolution. Doctrine cannot change from one thing into another. The Fathers were firm in fidelity to the deposit they had received, and that deposit could not be contradicted.

Modern people, especially Americans, prize *innovation*, *originality*, and *novelty*. But the Fathers were of a decidedly different cast of mind. When they wanted to insult or upbraid a churchman, they would call him an "innovator." Basil the Great once complimented a man by saying he "produced nothing of his own, no discovery of modern thought, but . . . he knew how to bring forth out of the hidden and goodly treasures of his heart the oldest of the store."[2]

We Christians are a spiritual temple built of living stones on the foundation of the apostles and prophets, with Christ Jesus as the cornerstone (Ephesians 2:20). We must rest firmly on what has come before, but we must take our place where no stone has rested before. To shift to the right or the left would be to cause the temple's wall to lean and collapse, bringing down the whole edifice. At the same time, we do no good if we fixate on the past and simply line ourselves up exactly with the stones in the last row. That, too, makes for a weak wall, prone to falling and not promoting stability for the rows to come after us. We have to find our proper place. It must be distinctively *ours*, in God's Providence, but it must be *proper*, in the great tradition.

———

The life of any family is preserved and handed on in many ways. My family was musical, so I learned to associate my parents' personal history with certain popular songs of their youth. That's the way they remembered their past; it had a soundtrack. My grandmother would often deliver a spiritual or moral lesson just by singing a phrase or a verse from a hymn.

Music is a powerful medium for memory—more reliable than a flash drive and vaster than the data cloud. I believe that music has always been among the great vessels of both tradition and development.

For most of history, perhaps, most Christians have been illiterate, yet they embraced the faith, practiced the faith, loved the faith, and taught the faith to their children. Many of them didn't have opportunities to learn it from books. The great theological studies written by Irenaeus, Athanasius, and Augustine were eagerly consumed by Church professionals—bishops, priests, monks, and nuns—and were then distilled into homilies and manuals. But few people in the congregations would ever have a chance to handle the source texts themselves. Parishes didn't have lending libraries, websites, or even a Sunday bulletin. These are largely unhelpful for a nonreading congregation.

The surest way for doctrine to enter minds and hearts—and stay there—was through music. This was true from the beginning. Think of Saint Paul in his prison cell with his companions. They were surrounded by unbelievers and hardened criminals, who were probably not terribly interested in what Paul had to say, yet "about midnight Paul and Silas were praying and singing hymns to God, *and the prisoners were listening to them*" (Acts 16:25). Sometimes, when exhortations hit a wall, melodies get a pass.

Paul knew that music would be an effective medium of transmission, so he told the next generation to make it so: "Let the word of Christ dwell in you richly, teach and admonish one another in all wisdom, and *sing psalms and hymns and spiritual songs* with thankfulness in your hearts to God" (Colossians 3:16). Again, it's clear: Christians were not to stop at the admonition; they were to go on to sing it! They needed to make it memorable. And then do it once more, with feeling: "addressing one another in psalms and hymns and spiritual songs, singing and making melody to the Lord with all your heart" (Ephesians 5:19).

The Fathers were obedient to Paul's instruction; and so much of what we have received from them is music. Some of the most revered Fathers were not only great preachers, but also prolific hymnographers: Ephrem of Syria, Ambrose of Milan, Hilary of Poitiers, Romanus of Beirut, Venantius Fortunatus, John of Damascus. History has preserved as well the works of many minor and unknown songwriters. Some of them are true works of art, and some have only minimal literary value. But the mere survival of these texts is a testimony to the power of melodies to convey religious truth.

The Fathers often complained that the heretics succeeded in making converts because they set their heresies to better, more memorable music. Arius was notorious for this, and the Arians continued to win hearts even after their condemnation by the Council of Nicaea. It was only with the rise of good Catholic music—from men like Ephrem, Ambrose, and Hilary—that the Church began to prevail.

Arius's arguments were abstract and abstruse; so were the Church's counterarguments. All of these proofs, demonstrations, and syllogisms were remote from the grasp of ordinary people. The relevant theological books were inaccessible in every sense of the word.

I like to think that, among ordinary folks, the controversy played out as a battle of the bands. When the true doctrine entered the mind and heart—through music that was at least equal to that of the heretics—the Good News prevailed.

I don't mean to imply that fourth-century congregations were any better about singing than Catholic parishes are today. The Fathers had practically to plead with people to open their mouths and sing. Saint Jerome once urged his people: "Even if you're tone-deaf . . . if your works are good, your song is sweet to God. If you would serve Christ, don't worry about your voice, but concentrate on the good words you sing."[3]

To sing is to pray twice—and to evangelize and catechize many times over. What was true in the fourth century is still true today. We have heresies to overcome. We have ignorance to vanquish. There is no more effective way to do it than by singing.

Cantors, choir members, organists, and other leaders of music ministry—they all need to know this. They are continuing the work of the apostles and Fathers. They are magnifying the message of the Gospels and the councils. They are the humble but privileged instruments that God uses in our day for the work of maintaining the tradition and developing the faith. They are *tradents,* to use the traditional term, and champions of orthodoxy.

———

It is good to belong to such a family, with such a tradition, where bishops have their important place, but so do the tone-deaf folks singing in the back pew.

The Church existed for centuries before the sacred documents were accepted as the single, universal book we call the New Testament. That final setting of the canon was a work of the Church, relying on tradition. It was not an easy call. *More than half* of the books we now accept as canonical were hardly mentioned at all before the third century. The earliest Fathers seem to have been unaware of them. And some of the sacred books were rejected outright by local churches: the Epistle to the Hebrews, the Epistle of James, the Second Epistle of Peter, the Second and Third Epistles of John, the Epistle of Jude, and the book of Revelation. While those inspired books were sometimes rejected, other books—including some of the earliest writings of the Fathers—were included in many local canons of Scripture.

Yet the tradition produced those books, tested them, and bore them along, conserving them in the great Church, which confirmed them definitively when the time was right for doing so, at the end of the fourth century.

The New Testament canon was a development, late in coming, but grounded in the tradition. Scripture is the earliest written record of apostolic tradition, and is the "canon," or "measuring stick," of all later expressions. Scripture is born from apostolic tradition, and guides apostolic tradition; and both are interpreted through the successors to the apostles and Peter, to whom was given the primacy. Without this threefold support—of Scripture, tradition, and magisterium—the stool of the Church would not stand upright. Take away any one of them, and the stability of the Church that authentically transmits the Gospel of Jesus Christ to the world in any era is threatened.

Only God could calibrate life so precisely—so that development never degenerates into mere progressivism and tradition never degenerates into mere traditionalism.

That's life in the household of the Fathers, the Church of the Christ. And it's something worth singing about.

Chapter 12

ON THE ROAD AGAIN

T SEEMED CLEAR TO ME, ALL THROUGH MY ADULT life, that God was calling me to "come to the quiet." That's how I put it in one of my album titles. I believed that as I grew older, my life would more and more resemble the stability of a monk who had his cell and nothing more.

The fire changed all that. When our common building burned, our community faced the necessary but seemingly impossible task of rebuilding. Insurance would take us part of the way, but just a small part, really.

I had become a "father." My titles in our little family are Founder, General Minister, and Spiritual Father, and the last is most important because it is familial.

A father who had partly retired would know what to do in similar circumstances. He would need to find income-producing work to support the family while it worked its way back to its proper place. As I prayed about the situation, God led me to a surprising new phase of my vocation.

I would return to touring, but not in the way that I had toured in the long-ago past. I would tour not concert halls and sports arenas. And I wouldn't just plug in and amplify.

I would tour in ministry. God was driving me from my

comfort zone, the life I'd known and loved. He was leading me from my hermitage and my habits. He was leading me out of the beautiful silence into which I had settled.

I knew why—in an immediate sense. Our family had bills to pay, and fathers need to take care of that as they can, even as they encourage their children to contribute what *they* can. My time on the road would give community members a chance to take more direct responsibility for the day-to-day operation of the monastery.

But there was the bigger *why,* the vocational *why.* Why would God lead me to meet him in silence, and to know him there, only—as soon as I was settled—to push me back out into the noise of highways and cities, setup and talking and tear-down.

I knew that my call would be to tell the world about the life-style we led at Little Portion. But there was a certain irony even in that. I would travel thousands of miles of interstate highways in order to promote stability and community. I would speak without ceasing about the virtues of silence and contemplation.

I had to laugh. I needed to pray. And, going back to my usual sources, I looked for models of such a wandering, preaching life. Scripture, of course, was replete with them. I faced the caution-ary tale of Jonah, and I knew that turning away from the proc-lamation was not an option. Yet I also began to see the relation between my years of relative silence and the intense period of activity that lay ahead. My time in the belly of the whale was necessary preparation for my future—and penance for my past.

The apostolic generation gave me many more examples. In-deed, the entire Church of Jerusalem (except the apostles) found itself scattered (Acts 8:1) because of persecution. The persecutors intended to drive them into silence, but instead they drove them into mission. The subsequent chapters of Church history are the stories of the spread of the Gospel "throughout the region of Judea and Samaria" and then as far as Antioch in Syria.

The apostles themselves had a peripatetic ministry, following the Spirit from place to place. Scripture shows Paul roaming through Asia and into Europe, preaching the Good News and planting churches. Tradition informs us that Thomas made it to India and ministered there for many years; believers in Kerala still call themselves "Thomas Christians." Peter, of course, made it to Rome. John was exiled to Patmos, where he received his divine Revelation.

Nor were these the only ones to rack up the miles. They were followed and accompanied in their wandering ways by Barnabas, Silas, John Mark, Luke, Prisca, Aquila, and others.

They all took their lead from the Son of Man, who had "nowhere to lay his head" (Matthew 8:20). Jesus himself spent much of his ministry "on tour," preaching and healing in towns, cities, and countryside—in Judea, Galilee, and even apostate Samaria—as well as from a boat on a lake!

The Fathers, in turn, looked to the Lord's example and followed it well. Sometimes their itinerancy was chosen. Sometimes it was thrust upon them. It was there, however, from the beginning.

The *Didache* records a transitional period in the Church's life. Chapter 11 seems to address a historical moment when the churches were still served by wandering "prophets."

Whosoever, therefore, comes and teaches you all these things that have been said before, receive him. . . . Let every apostle who comes to you be received as the Lord. But he shall not remain more than one day or two days. [1]

Later chapters, however, assume a stable local clergy, "bishops and deacons worthy of the Lord."[2]

Nevertheless, we know that some of the bishops found themselves itinerant by necessity, and they made the blessed most of it. Think of Ignatius! His death sentence in the late first or early second century required him to sojourn under armed guard from Antioch to Rome. Travel was arduous and slow. His military escort probably had other business to conduct along the way. And so they stopped in many major cities along the route. Ignatius wasted no opportunities; he met with the local Christians, met with their bishops, and wrote letters to the churches. Wherever he found himself, he knew what God wanted him to do.

A few years later, Justin Martyr, a philosopher and layman, chose to follow a similar path to Rome. Along the way, he brought the "philosophy" of Jesus Christ to the gathering places of the cities, just as Paul had done among the intellectuals in Athens.

As I read the trusted sources, it became clear to me that the path to which God was calling me was, as ever, an ancient path. My challenge would be to integrate the silence of the contemplative life with the bustle of the months and years ahead.

—

Ages ago, long before I was Catholic, when I was taking my first steps in the Jesus Movement, I had a moment in prayer when I saw myself walking from place to place in simplicity, bringing the Gospel. I was given to understand that this would be the culmination of my work on earth. I did not know what it meant, and I am still puzzling it out. But I have long since learned to trust the Lord to lead me.

In the years since the fire, I have typically spent a hundred and fifty evenings addressing crowds of people in parishes. The congregations are usually mixed—some Catholic, some Protestant, some seekers. I talk to them about the Scriptures and about our friends Diadochus, Ignatius, Chrysostom, and Augustine. I teach them to pray the Jesus Prayer. I walk them through the Church's ancient liturgy. My community and I rely on the free-will offerings given at these events; and we have not been disappointed by the generosity of people who come to hear me.

Many of these events last only one night, but the full presentation, as I prefer to give it, lasts for three nights. We also produced a three-disk video of the presentation, titled *Nothing Is Impossible with God*. This enabled me to reach even into the out-of-the-way corners that had no parish church to shelter me. We aired all three segments as part of the *Live with Passion* program on the Church Channel—and they caught the attention of the folks at Trinity Broadcasting Network. TBN is a vast and well-established evangelical media ministry with more than forty years of history. TBN invited me to appear on their *Praise the Lord* program, which goes out to hundreds of millions of people. Soon afterward, they offered me an opportunity to tape my own regular show. *All Things Are Possible* began airing weekly in 2014.

So when I'm not sitting in a parish somewhere, I'm usually on my way to one, trying to make the best use possible of America's system of interstate highways. For me, the ancient path these days looks a lot like the freeways of Southern California and the Beltway around Washington, D.C.

Yet it is the same. I follow after John Cassian who journeyed from the Egyptian desert to teach the men and women of Gaul (modern-day France) to live like true ascetics. I follow after the Irish monks who saved civilization by taking classic faith and classical learning back to Europe, the continent that had let these treasures slip away.

I follow Brendan the Navigator, that sixth-century monk who followed the Lord's command to "put out into the deep" (Luke 5:4) and in the process—some people believe—discovered America.

I have no such delusions of grandeur. I want, however, to do what I can to help America discover what I have seen, and known, and wept to love: the beauty of Jesus Christ, the rock of his Church, the glory of his tradition.

Chapter 13

THE GOD-BEARER

LATE IN LIFE I FIND MYSELF ADJUSTING, ONCE again, to sleeping in strange places and eating where I can find my meals. As I said in the last chapter, I've sought out companions for my journey in the Scriptures and among the saints, but one has proven more steadfast and helpful than all the others. I am, after all, trying to do in a small way what she did first.

By the grace of God, Mary brought God into the world. The early Fathers called her *Theotokos*, God-bearer. I, too, am trying to bear him with me.

She was no stranger to the road. No sooner had she conceived her divine Child than she was traveling on a mission of service to help her kinswoman Elizabeth, who lived in Judea's hill country. As Mary's date approached, she made the arduous journey from Nazareth to Bethlehem, because the authorities insisted that every family be enrolled. Soon after she gave birth, she had to take flight to distant Egypt to protect her Son from those who would kill him. Later she made the long return trip home. When Jesus began his ministry, she followed him, even to the foot of the cross, where she watched him die. As he rose, she took her place with the Church, where she remains. According to ancient tradition, she went with the apostle John to Ephesus, where she spent her final years. Christians still venerate the spot where she may have lived; good sisters keep a church there, welcoming pilgrims from all over the world.

Mary was a traveler, a wanderer, a sojourner, but she never ceased to be a God-bearer. That was not a phase in her life. It was her life. It was her identity, though she needed to live it differently according to the different circumstances she faced.

I've decided I must learn from her. She has been my teacher and guide in this new phase of life.

———

Converts can be a bit frightening. Some embrace with almost fanatical zeal the things that lifelong Catholics find commonplace. Their faith radiates in a glory cloud of rosaries, scapulars, and prayer cards. But that's not the way it worked for me.

By the time I was baptized, I had long since established the personal habit of testing everything against the Scriptures, and I did it instinctively. So I took up Catholic customs very slowly and methodically, but over time I got to all of them.

The most alien, perhaps, was the special honor that Catholics pay to the Blessed Virgin Mary. But what I soon discovered was that such devotion should not be alien to a Christian who walks the ancient path. In fact, I learned slowly that the Church's devotion to Mary historically grew in direct proportion to its appreciation of the incarnation of the Word in Jesus Christ, Mary's Son. I accepted this intellectually soon after my conversion, but it has taken years for this to grow into a heartfelt love and devotion to Mary, who always points toward Jesus.

The evangelists could not proclaim the Gospel without her. She plays the dominant speaking part in the first two chapters of Saint Luke's Gospel, and she seems to have been one of his major sources. In Saint John's Gospel, she launches Jesus's ministry with her simple observation that the hosts of the wedding feast had run out of wine. As the fourth evangelist stands at the foot of the cross, he stands beside the mother of Jesus (John 19:25-27). In fact, as Saint Matthew and Saint Mark show, she had always remained with Jesus, following him in his peripatetic mission (Matthew 12:46; Mark 3:31).

On the cross, Jesus said to his Beloved Disciple, "Behold, your mother" (John 19:27), and ever afterward Jesus's beloved disciples have found their place with her, in the household of God. When we first see the Church gathered after Jesus's ascension into heaven, it is gathered in prayer "together with . . . Mary the mother of Jesus" (Acts 1:14).

When Saint Paul gave his most compact summary of the Gospel, he knew he had to include her: "when the time had fully come, God sent forth his Son, born of woman, born under the law" (Galatians 4:4).

When Saint John saw heaven, he saw the Mother of the Messiah crowned with stars (Revelation 12:1-5).

Mary was an alien presence in my life as I made the transition from the Jesus Movement to the Church. But why? I should have detected her quiet presence in the Scriptures—her persistence in interceding at Cana, her steadfastness in following her Son, her constant focus on God, and her simple, but eminently useful spiritual direction: "Do whatever he tells you" (John 2:5).

Maybe it was because she was so quiet, and I—at least in

my Jesus Movement phase—was always ready with an argument backed up by twenty proof texts. While I was reaching into God's Word for artillery and ammunition, I missed her quiet but constant virginal presence.

Her very goodness likely worked against her. She is the only major figure in the New Testament who doesn't show a shadow side. Peter is passionate but unreliable. Paul is bold, but he can also be temperamental and grudging. Thomas is inquisitive, but sometimes he lets skepticism get the better of him.

Mary never intrudes on the drama with sins and faults. When she appears, she edifies.

I noticed this as I read more in the works of the Fathers. Like Saint Paul and the evangelists, they found it impossible to proclaim the Gospel without at least mentioning her. It's not that they were writing treatises on Mariology, but they considered her to be a key part of the story of Jesus Christ. She was an essential detail in God's revelation to humanity.

In the first century, already, there were misinformed Christians who wished to deny Jesus's true humanity or his true divinity. For Ignatius of Antioch, Mary was a safeguard of both, so he mentions her often. He tells the Ephesians that Jesus was "from Mary and from God."[1] He was "conceived by Mary of the seed of David, but also by the Holy Spirit."[2] To the Smyrnaeans Ignatius emphasized that Jesus was "truly born of a virgin."[3]

In the next generation, Saint Justin Martyr presents Mary as the New Eve. The Virgin Mary's obedience is the undoing of the Virgin Eve's disobedience.[4] This theme emerges again in the teaching of Irenaeus of Lyons, the disciple of Polycarp, the disciple of John, who says poetically that Mary's obedience "untied the knot" of Eve's sin. "What Eve bound through her unbelief, Mary loosened by her faith."[5]

The tender devotion that we find in the writings of the Fathers is reflected in the simple prayers of the time. In the sands of Egypt, archaeologists recently found a scrap of papyrus from the early third century bearing a prayer the Church still recites today: "We fly to your patronage, O holy Mother of God. . . ."

The graffiti in the Roman catacombs echoes this devotion, and the earliest Christian artworks portray it. Mary's visage appears on medals, lamps, and flasks from ancient times. Her feasts appeared on the calendars of churches in fourth-century Jerusalem, Constantinople, Egypt, and Syria.

She is a recurring presence, but still quiet. Not until the fourth and fifth centuries, when heretics made full frontal assaults on Jesus's humanity and divinity, did the Fathers begin to develop a Mariology. It first emerged in Athanasius and Ephrem in the East, Ambrose and Augustine in the West, but then suddenly it was everywhere, most especially in the works of Cyril of Alexandria, the great bishop and scholar of Scripture.

Cyril ardently defended Mary's title *Theotokos*—God-bearer, Mother of God—which was already hallowed by long tradition. Then, in the fifth century, some began to say that Mary should *not* be called God's mother because she did not precede God in time. She did not give birth to God, but only to Jesus—and not to his divinity, but only his humanity.

Cyril responded that Jesus's divinity was not separable from his humanity. Mothers give birth not to natures, but to persons; and the person of Jesus was both divine and human. Mary did not precede God in time, but she definitely mothered him in

Jesus. From the moment of her annunciation, she bore God in her womb.

To defend Mary's titles and prerogatives was to defend the truth about Jesus. Luke and John knew this instinctively, as did Ignatius and Irenaeus. They witnessed to the tradition that Cyril defended.

Reading the Fathers, I began to see what those men saw—and I saw that it was beautiful. I began to understand the beauty at the heart of Dante's *Paradiso,* Michelangelo's *Pietà,* and Bach's "Ave Maria." In my own devotion, I gave it expression in songs of my own, such as "Holy Is His Name."

That song has been sung by millions of people around the world—at grand papal events and in humble parishes. It is perhaps another of God's beautiful ironies: that a song about Mary should be the most popular composition by a convert from the Jesus Movement.

It is proper to speak of Mary in a book about the Fathers, and not only because they spoke about her first, but also because she is the model of all the redeemed, and she always points the way to her Son, Jesus. It is the Fathers who reveal a developed understanding and devotion to Mary, the Mother of Jesus, our Lord and God. She is the God-bearer. She also proclaims and magnifies by her holy humility and sacred silence how you and I are to be bearers of God by bringing Jesus into this world every day. We do this by means of the living tradition. We do this by placing the stone of our life into the spiritual temple of the Church. But she is always there to remind us that Jesus holds the whole structure together. "Do whatever he tells you." We can do nothing on our own. This remains the constant message of the Fathers, as it is the message of Mary's life.

I am bearing God, and so I can learn to be alone with him, even in cities like Los Angeles, Portland, Des Moines, and Wichita.

I am learning from the God-bearer, whom the Scriptures portray as almost constantly in motion—yet constantly in contemplation.

"She . . . considered in her mind what sort of greeting this might be" (Luke 1:29).

"Mary kept all these things, pondering them in her heart" (Luke 2:19).

"And . . . his mother kept all these things in her heart" (Luke 2:51).

Mary was the exemplar for the active saints, but also for the contemplative saints. She was the first embodiment of the way that Saint Augustine judged to be best of all, the life that is both active and contemplative. He said: "The love of truth seeks a holy leisure, the demands of charity undertake an honest toil."[6]

So in going this way with Mary, I am going the way of the Fathers, but also the way of most Christians in every age. We are God-bearers, and we cannot bear him faithfully unless we contemplate him lovingly. Like any love, the love of God requires time. Like any love, it requires conversation, and that means regular prayer. Like any love, divine love seeks union, and that means a deep sacramental life.

My way is probably much like yours. I am called to be a contemplative in the middle of the city. I am called to know stillness even though I'm busy. You and I live in a time of great anxiety and stress. We sense that our world is changing from something we once knew to something unfamiliar. Well, the

Fathers give us hope for such a time. They managed the transition with fidelity. They refused to be changed by the world, and they changed it instead, even as the world persecuted them and put them to death.

Still, the faith of our Fathers prevailed, and it's living still.

Post-Christian paganism looks a lot like pre-Christian paganism. As we read the Fathers, we come to recognize the story line. The devil's tricks don't change much. And God's arm has not been shortened.

In the Fathers' victory—over Rome, over vice, over self, over Satan—we see our own, because our victory, like theirs, belongs to Jesus. "He himself brought death to nought," Athanasius proclaimed, "and every day raises monuments to his victory in his own disciples."[7]

Glory be to God in all things!

Timeline

Many dates are approximate.

First Century

c. 48 to c. 120	The *Didache*
c. 50 to c. 90	The writings of the New Testament
c. 64	Death of Peter and Paul under Nero
c. 67 or c. 97	Clement of Rome, Letter to the Corinthians
c. 80–100	Letter of Barnabas
c. 107	Death of Ignatius of Antioch
c. 105–155	Ministry of Polycarp of Smyrna
c. 135–168	Activity of Justin Martyr
c. 170–202	Ministry of Irenaeus of Lyons
c. 189–215	Teaching of Clement of Alexandria
c. 197–225	Apologetics of Tertullian
248–258	Ministry of Cyprian of Carthage
203–254	Origen's teaching career
250	Brutal Decian persecution begins
303–311	Diocletian's persecution—the bloodiest
306–337	Rise and reign of Constantine the Great
313	Christianity legalized in Roman Empire
325	Council of Nicaea condemns Arianism
325–372	Ministry of Athanasius the Great
362–379	Ministry of Basil the Great

367	First appearance of the New Testament canon as known today
374–397	Ministry of Ambrose of Milan
379–420	Ministry of Jerome
361–390	Ministry of Gregory of Nazianzus
381	Council of Constantinople
371–395	Ministry of Gregory of Nyssa
391–430	Ministry of Augustine of Hippo
393, 397	New Testament canon approved at Synods of Hippo & Carthage
431	Council of Ephesus
451	Council of Chalcedon
c. 570–632	Life of Muhammad
579–604	Ministry of Gregory the Great
c. 600–662	Activity of Maximus the Confessor
749	Death of John of Damascus, last of the Eastern Fathers

Notes

Preface

1. Pope Francis, *Evangelii Gaudium* (apostolic exhortation, On the Proclamation of the Gospel in Today's World), November 24, 2013, 3.

Chapter 1: You Can Become All Fire

1. Benedicta Ward, SG, ed. and tr., *The Sayings of the Desert Fathers: The Alphabetical Collection* (Kalamazoo, MI: Cistercian Publications, 1984), 103.

Chapter 2: Our Spiritual Fathers

1. This is not to overlook motherhood. Mary is honored as the greatest saint. But that is beyond the scope of this book.
2. Polycarp, *Letter to the Philippians* 7.1-2.
3. See the account of their meeting in Saint Irenaeus of Lyons, *Against the Heresies* 3.3.4.
4. Saint Vincent of Lérins, *Commonitorium* 4.3.
5. Ibid., *Commonitorium* 28.72.

CHAPTER 3: JESUS CHRIST

1. Saint Ignatius of Antioch, *Letter to the Romans* 4.
2. Saint Irenaeus of Lyon, *Against the Heresies* 3.21.9.
3. See ibid., *Against the Heresies* 5.14.1.
4. Saint Jerome, *Prologue to the Commentary on Isaiah.*
5. See Saint Ignatius of Antioch, *Letter to the Smyrnaeans* 8 and *Martyrdom of Polycarp* 8, 16, and 19.
6. Saint Ignatius of Antioch, *Letter to the Ephesians* 1 and 18.2; *Letter to the Romans* 1.
7. Ibid., *Letter to the Romans* 7.
8. Ibid., *Letter to the Smyrnaeans* 7.
9. Ibid., *Letter to the Romans* 7.
10. Ibid., *Letter to the Smyrnaeans* 6-7.
11. Ibid.
12. Pliny the Younger, *Letters*, Book 10, 96.
13. Saint Cyprian of Carthage, *Exhortation to Martyrdom* 6.
14. Tertullian, *On Prayer* 3.
15. Aidan Nichols, O. P., *The Shape of Catholic Theology* (Collegeville, MN: The Liturgical Press, 1991), 205–6.
16. John Henry Newman, *An Essay on the Development of Christian Doctrine* (London: Longmans, Green, 1909), 8.

CHAPTER 4: SALVATION

1. See Enrico Mazza, *The Origins of the Eucharistic Prayer* (Collegeville, MN: Pueblo, 1995), 40–41; also, Clayton Jefford, *The Apostolic Fathers and the New Testament* (Peabody, MA: Hendrickson, 2006), 20.
2. *Letter of Barnabas* 11.11.
3. Tertullian, *On Baptism* 12.
4. Saint Ignatius of Antioch, *Ephesians* 20.
5. *The Habit of Being: Letters of Flannery O'Connor*, selected and edited by Sally Fitzgerald (New York: Vintage, 1979), 125. All

the sacraments are signs, but not *merely* signs. They are signs that bring about what they signify. O'Connor was responding to the novelist Mary McCarthy, who accepted the Eucharist only as a symbol, damning it with faint praise.

6. Saint Irenaeus of Lyons, *Against the Heresies* 3.17.1-3.
7. The best introduction to this particular doctrine of the Fathers is Daniel A. Keating, *Deification and Grace* (Naples, FL: Sapientia Press, 2007). For a broad ecumenical treatment, from Protestant, Catholic, and Orthodox authors, see Michael J. Christensen and Jeffery A. Wittung, eds., *Partakers of the Divine Nature: The History and Development of Deification in the Christian Traditions* (Grand Rapids, MI: Baker, 2007).
8. Saint Irenaeus of Lyons, *Against the Heresies* 3.19.1.
9. Ibid., *Against the Heresies,* preface to Book 5.
10. Saint Athanasius of Alexandria, *On the Incarnation of the Word* 54.3.
11. Pope Francis, *Evangelii Gaudium* 8.
12. Saint Augustine, *Sermons* 169.13.

CHAPTER 6: PRAYER OF THE HEART

1. Pope Saint John Paul II, *Redemptoris Mater* (encyclical On the Blessed Virgin Mary in the Life of the Pilgrim Church), March 25, 1987, 34.
2. Pope Saint John Paul II, *Ut Unum Sint* (encyclical On Commitment to Ecumenism), May 25, 1995, 54.
3. Saint Diadochus of Photiki, *On Spiritual Knowledge* 59.
4. See Tertullian, *Against Hermogones* 3.

CHAPTER 7: THE PUBLIC WORK

1. Saint Ignatius of Antioch, *Letter to the Philadelphians* 4.
2. See his *Homilies on First Corinthians* 36.4-6.

3. See Robert F. Taft, S.J., *Through Their Own Eyes: Liturgy as the Byzantines Saw It* (Berkeley, CA: InterOrthodox Press, 2006), 77.

4. Tertullian, *On the Resurrection of the Flesh* 61.

5. Ibid., *De Corona* 3.

6. Saint Cyril of Jerusalem, *Catechetical Lectures* 13.36.

7. Saint Ignatius of Antioch, *Letter to the Smyrnaeans* 7.

8. Ibid., *Letter to the Ephesians* 1.

9. Saint Justin Martyr, *First Apology* 66.

10. Ibid., *First Apology* 65.

11. There's a lengthy discussion of these terms—and others—in E. B. Pusey, *The Doctrine of the Real Presence: As Contained in the Fathers* (London: John Henry Parker, 1855).

12. Pope Francis, *Evangelii Gaudium* 83.

CHAPTER 8: NOTHING WITHOUT THE BISHOP

1. *Didache* 9.

2. Saint Ignatius of Antioch, *Letter to the Magnesians* 7.

3. Saint Clement of Rome, *To the Corinthians* 42, 44.

4. Ibid., *Letter to the Corinthians* 44.

5. Saint Ignatius of Antioch, *Letter to the Ephesians* 4.1.

6. Ibid., *Letter to the Ephesians* 5.3.

7. Ibid., *Letter to the Magnesians* 3; see also *Letter to the Trallians* 3.

8. Ibid., *Letter to the Ephesians* 6.

9. Ibid., *Letter to the Smyrnaeans* 8.

10. Ibid., *Letter to the Trallians* 3.

11. Ibid., *Letter to the Philadelphians* 3.

12. For an excellent refutation of this position by a modern Protestant scholar, see Thomas A. Robinson, *Ignatius of Antioch and the Parting of the Ways* (Peabody, MA: Hendrickson, 2009), 99–102.

13. Eusebius, *Ecclesiastical History* 1.4.1, 1.4.15.

14. Saint Irenaeus of Lyons, *Against the Heresies* 3.3.4.

15. Ibid., *Against the Heresies* 4.33.8.
16. Ibid., *Against the Heresies* 3.3.2.
17. Saint Jerome, *Letters* 15.1.

CHAPTER 9: CHARITY

1. Tertullian, *Apologeticum* 39.
2. Saint Ignatius of Antioch, *Letter to the Smyrnaeans* 6-7.
3. *Didascalia Apostolorum,* quoted in Lucien Deiss, *Springtime of the Liturgy: Liturgical Texts of the First Four Centuries* (Collegeville, MN: Liturgical Press, 1979), 174.
4. John Chrysostom, *Homilies on the Gospel of Matthew* 50.4, as quoted in John Paul II, *Dies Domini,* Apostolic Letter on Keeping the Lord's Day Holy, July 5, 1998.
5. Benedicta Ward, tr. and ed., *The Sayings of the Desert Fathers,* rev. ed. (Kalamazoo, MI: Cistercian Publications, 1984), 24.

CHAPTER 10: STEWARDSHIP OF THE EARTH

1. I am not the first or the only author, of course, to have noticed the Fathers' usefulness in considering environmental ethics. See, for example, E. Kaniyamparambil, "Ecological Wisdom of the Patristic Tradition: An Analysis of the Human Relation to the Creation in the Light of the Present Ecological Crisis," in *Indian Journal of Spirituality* 14 (2011): 52–81; and Jame Schaefer, *Theological Foundations for Environmental Ethics: Reconstructing Patristic and Medieval Concepts* (Washington, DC: Georgetown University Press, 2009).
2. Saint Gregory of Nazianzus, *Orations* 43.63.
3. Brothers and Sisters of Charity, *Rule, Constitution, and Directory: Monastic and Domestic* (Berryville, AR: Little Portion Hermitage, 2012), 130.
4. Pope Saint Clement of Rome, *Letter to the Corinthians* 20.
5. Saint Basil the Great, *On the Holy Spirit* 8.18.

6. See Stacy Trasancos, "Father Jaki and the Stillbirths of Science," in *St. Austin Review*, May/June 2014, online at staustinreview.com.
7. Pope Saint Clement of Rome, *Letter to the Corinthians* 20.
8. Saint Gregory of Nyssa, *De Hominis Opificio* 4 (a treatise on Genesis).
9. Pope Saint John Paul II, *Evangelium Vitae* (encyclical On the Value and Inviolability of Human Life), March 25, 1995, 52.
10. Saint Basil the Great, *To the Rich* 7.
11. Ibid.
12. Saint John Chrysostom, *Homilies on First Corinthians* 15.14.
13. Saint Basil the Great, "I Will Tear Down My Barns," n. 1, in *On Social Justice* (Crestwood, NY: St. Vladimir's Seminary Press, 2009), 61.
14. I recommend especially two collections in the Popular Patristics Series of Saint Vladimir Seminary Press: Saint Basil the Great, *On Social Justice* (Yonkers, NY: St. Vladimir's Seminary Press, 2009); and Saint John Chrysostom, *On Wealth and Poverty* (Yonkers, NY: St. Vladimir's Seminary Press, 1999). Also good for meditation is *On Living Simply: The Golden Voice of John Chrysostom* (Liguori, MO: Triumph, 1996).

CHAPTER 11: HEART AND HANDS AND VOICES

1. Saint Basil the Great, *Letters* 223.3, translation in Philip Rousseau's excellent biography *Basil of Caesarea* (Berkeley, CA: University of California Press, 1994), 23.
2. Saint Basil the Great, *Letters* 28.1.
3. Saint Jerome, *Commentary on Ephesians* (5:19).

CHAPTER 12: ON THE ROAD AGAIN

1. *Didache* 11.
2. *Didache* 15.

CHAPTER 13: THE GOD-BEARER

1. Saint Ignatius of Antioch, *Letter to the Ephesians* 7.
2. Ibid., *Letter to the Ephesians* 18.
3. Ibid., *Letter to the Smyrnaeans* 1.1.
4. Saint Justin Martyr, *Dialogue with Trypho* 100.
5. Saint Irenaeus of Lyons, *Against the Heresies* 3.22.4.
6. Saint Augustine of Hippo, *City of God* 19.19.
7. Saint Athanasius the Great, *On the Incarnation of the Word* 5.29.